The Positive Classroom Method

5 Steps to a Smooth-Running Classroom

Muriel K. Rand

Illustrations by Catherine L. Rand

Copyright ©2014 Princeton Square Press. All rights reserved.

Illustrations Copyright ©2012-14 Catherine L. Rand

Published by Princeton Square Press
301 N. Harrison St. No. 312
Princeton, NJ 08536

No part of this publication may be reproduced, stored in a retrieval system, or transmitted in any form or by any means, electronic, mechanical, photocopying, recording, scanning, or otherwise, except as permitted under Section 107 or 108 of the 1976 United States Copyright Act, without either the prior written permission of the publisher, except by a reviewer who may quote brief passages in a review.

ISBN-13: 978-0-9882766-5-9

To all my student teachers who have taught me what good classroom management means

Contents

- Introduction 1
- **Step One: Teach Procedures** 3
  - *Plan the Procedures Throughout the Day* 3
  - *Attention Please!* 8
  - *Create Smooth Transitions* 8
  - *Get the Children into Routines* 11
  - *Step One Checklist for Teaching Procedures* 13
- **Step 2: Build Classroom Community** 15
  - *Help Children Feel They Belong* 15
  - *Use Community Building Activities* 17
  - *Create Classroom Rules* 20
  - *Help Children to Live by Classroom Rules* 22
  - *Use Positive Teacher Responses* 22
  - *Step 2 Checklist for Building a Community of Learners* 24
- **Step 3: Teach Classroom Success Skills** 25
  - *Teach Children to Regulate their Behavior* 25
  - *Teach Children to Control Emotions* 28
  - *Teach Children to Calm Down* 30
  - *Teach Academic Survival Skills* 34
  - *Teaching Peer Relationship Skills* 37
  - *Step 3 Checklist for Teaching Classroom Success Skills* 41
- **Step 4: Engage Children in Learning** 43
  - *Make Whole-Group Lessons Effective* 43
  - *Use Alternatives to Hand Raising* 44
  - *Make Seatwork Successful* 47
  - *Make Sharing Time and Group Discussions Effective* 48
  - *Replace Whole-Group Activities with Learning Centers* 49
  - *Plan Learning Center Activities* 50
  - *Be Prepared* 55
  - *Step 4 Checklist for Engaging Children in Learning* 55
- **Step 5: Guide Children's Behavior** 57

Only Respond as Much as Necessary *57*
Teach Children to Resolve Conflicts *58*
Stop Using Time Out *61*
Use a Quiet Corner *61*
Set and Enforce Limits *62*
Use Natural Consequences *63*
Use Exclusion when Appropriate *64*
Use Deprivation When Appropriate *64*
Use Restitution When Appropriate *65*
Help Attention-Seeking Children *66*
Understand and Intervene in the Acting-Out Cycle *68*
Step 5 Checklist for Guiding Behavior *73*
Find Joy in Teaching *73*

REFERENCES AND RESOURCES **75**
About the Author *85*
About the Illustrator *85*

Introduction

The Positive Classroom Method includes five steps that create a smooth-running classroom. These steps will not only help your children learn better and achieve more—they will also help save your sanity and find more joy in teaching.

Good classroom management requires a process that helps children meet their basic needs. There is not one strategy or technique that will create a positive classroom, but rather an entire system that comes together with five steps:

> Step 1: Teach Procedures
>
> Step 2: Build Classroom Community
>
> Step 3: Teach School Success Skills
>
> Step 4: Engage Children in Learning
>
> Step 5: Guide Children's Behavior

If you are a new teacher, these steps will be the basis for developing your classroom management. If you are an experienced teacher, think about which of these areas that could use improvement as you review the five steps. Throughout this book are links to more information on The Positive Classroom Blog and other websites which includes videos, images, and ideas from around the Internet. With these strategies in place, you will have more time to teach, more time for children to discover, play, experiment, and learn. You will create a positive classroom!

Step One: Teach Procedures

A smooth running classroom depends on children knowing the procedures so well that they don't have to be told. Teaching procedures takes some time and energy, especially at the beginning of the year, but it is crucial for preventing behavior problems and improving the efficiency of learning.

In a well-functioning classroom, the children enter each morning and are greeted by the teacher. They all know exactly how to put away their things, and what they should do next. The children get involved in activities right away. The atmosphere is relaxed and there is little wasted time. Throughout the day, the children know the routines so well they do most of them automatically. The teacher gives a few reminders and consistently gives positive feedback to children who are on track and doing what will help them learn and develop. There is very little off-task behavior, and no nagging or cajoling. The true test of good procedures is that the children stay on task even if the teacher is out of the room or involved in another activity.

Plan the Procedures Throughout the Day

The first step in teaching procedures is to think through the parts of the day and make a list or description of the different procedures you want to establish. Write down what behavior you would expect from the children. For example, if you were teaching 2nd grade, you would want to establish a procedure for when children first enter the classroom with the following steps:

1. Come into the classroom and walk over to the coat hooks.
2. Look around and make sure there is space between you and the other children.
3. Take off your coat and hang it on the hook.
4. Bring your book bag to your desk. Take out any papers for the teacher and put them on the corner of your desk.
5. Sit down and look at the board for "Do Now" work.
6. Begin work.

Close your eyes and picture the children engaging in the activity or transition. What do you want them to be doing? What does the classroom look like and sound like? Where are the children going to? What steps need to be taken? Next, teach the children this routine until they know it well enough to do it automatically. Don't think that teaching the procedures once is ever enough. This will probably require that you teach and re-teach many times, as well as give supportive reminders while children practice this routine.

The best way to teach routines is to have the children actually do them as a lesson. The Responsive Classroom (Wilson, 2012) has a wonderful strategy for teaching procedures called Interactive Modeling.

Interactive Modeling has four steps:
1. You explain why the procedure is important.
2. Students observe the model.
3. Students describe what's happening.
4. Students practice and get immediate feedback.

> ### *Interactive Modeling Example: Getting Ready for Lunch*
>
> 1. At the beginning of the day, gather the children and talk about why it is important to be organized and ready for lunch.
>
> 2. Demonstrate how they should put their books away, push in their chair, get their lunch from their cubby if they brought one and line up by the door. Ask them what they noticed.
>
> 3. Next have them practice these same steps. Have them pretend to be working, then ring the chime and ask them to get ready for lunch. Give positive feedback to the children who are responding appropriately. You could say, "I noticed that some people put their book away and pushed in their chairs. I saw many of you line up quietly and calmly."
>
> 4. If not all the children responded appropriately, practice again, pointing out those who are following the procedures. If anyone is still not following, you can say, "I see some people who are not quite getting it yet. Who can model what we should do?" Have a couple of children model it again, then ask the group what they notice. Once again, have them practice and give feedback.

If children are not following the routines, re-teach them and provide more practice. Teachers with the smoothest running classrooms spend the first six weeks of the school year focusing primarily on teaching procedures and developing routines. This time is more than made up for with the increase in efficiency throughout the year.

Use concrete descriptions of expected behaviors. Young children do not understand abstractions like "be polite" or "listen" so your directions need to be put into behavioral terms. For example, what specifically do children need to do to "be polite"? One way to do this is with the use of a graphic organizer called a "T-Chart" (because it looks like the letter T). For example, what does it look like to be polite? What does it sound like? Our chart might look like this:

Be Polite	
Looks Like:	Sounds Like:
» Smiling » Holding the door » Looking at who is talking » Helping someone pick things up » Leaving space around people » Shaking hands	» "Good Morning" » Friendly Voices » "Nice job!" » "Can I help you?" » "Please stop, I don't like that" » "Excuse me"

Interactive Modeling Worksheet

Procedure to be taught: _____

Step 1. Explain why this procedure important

Step 2: Model the procedure

Step 3: Ask what the children noticed about what you modeled

Step 4: Have children practice the procedure and give positive feedback

Step 5: Repeat modeling and noticing if necessary

T-Chart for Behavior:

Looks Like:	Sounds Like:

Classroom Procedures Checklist

- ☐ Arrival: putting things away
- ☐ Signing in
- ☐ Morning announcements
- ☐ Signal for getting the children's attention
- ☐ Going to the bathroom/washing hands/getting a drink
- ☐ Eating breakfast/lunch
- ☐ Signal for lowering the noise
- ☐ Moving from tables or desks to carpet for group time
- ☐ Sitting during group time
- ☐ Moving to learning centers
- ☐ Moving from group to working independently at desks/tables
- ☐ Cleaning up after centers
- ☐ Working with a partner
- ☐ Taking turns
- ☐ Fire drills/Lock down drills
- ☐ Leaving the classroom
- ☐ Walking in the halls
- ☐ Coming back into school/center/classroom
- ☐ What to do when teacher has phone call, visitor, etc.
- ☐ What to do when children finish early
- ☐ Putting things away in desk/taking them out
- ☐ Finding the page in the textbook
- ☐ Sharing materials
- ☐ Choosing a book in the class library
- ☐ Taking care of materials (putting caps on markers, etc)
- ☐ What to do when someone is hurt
- ☐ What to do when children need to calm down
- ☐ Getting things ready to go home
- ☐ Getting on the bus/meeting parent/going to aftercare

Attention Please!

On the first day of school, create a signal to get the children's attention and practice it again and again throughout the day. Sounds or lights are more effective than hand signals since children will not always be looking at you.

Depending upon the age of the child and your preferences, teach the steps the children should follow when you ring the bell or flick the lights. The steps might be something like:

1. Lips closed
2. Hands at your sides
3. Eyes on the teacher
4. Body still

As you practice this throughout the day in the first weeks of school, try to get across the message that this signal is important, but be light-hearted in teaching the children how to respond so they begin to associate good feelings with the quiet signal.

If you find the children are slow to respond, or are ignoring it, go back to your practice sessions. You can make it a challenge to see how quickly the children can get quiet and create a game-like attitude when you practice. As the school year goes on, you will still need to support children with positive reminders and perhaps play this modeling game a few more times until your signal becomes routine.

> *Special Tips:*
>
> 1. If you find the children are not responding quickly to your signal, stop and practice. ***Never*** talk over the children or allow them to chat while you speak. Simply review the expectations, without complaining or criticizing, and practice the quiet signal again.
> 2. Be sure to point out the children who are quiet and paying attention and give them positive feedback, rather than drawing attention to those who are off-task.

Create Smooth Transitions

Transitions are tough. All transitions go more smoothly if children know what to expect. Use interactive modeling to teach each transition. Practice these until the children know what they should be doing and can do it quickly and easily. Here are some tips for making transitions smoother:

Give warnings. This may seem obvious, but sometimes you lose track of the time and try to quickly get children to change what they are doing. Resist this! Stay organized and give the children at least one warning that a transition is coming up—more might be needed for children who have trouble with transitions. You can also use timers to let children know how much time is left before a transition. This can be a personal kitchen timer for an individual child, or a timer posted on your SmartBoard or computer screen which counts down for the whole class.

Use music cues. Music is a powerful way of helping children to know the schedule and the behaviors that are expected at different times. Plan welcome songs to begin the day, clean up songs, soft music before nap time or quiet activities, and a good-bye song at dismissal.

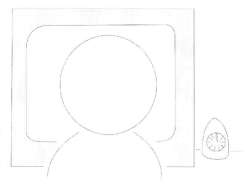

Actively supervise. During transitions, scan all areas of the room, moving to potential problem areas, making your presence known, and interacting with the children (McIntosh et al., 2004). If you are busy during transitions getting your materials ready for the next activity, talking to other adults in the room, or taking care of administrative work, the children will likely misbehave. Much research over many years has shown that effective teachers have the room and the work ready before school begins.

Allow time for transitions. Young children need plenty of time to figure out where they need to go or what they need to do next (Buck, 1999). Often teachers plan schedules that reflect the time they need for each activity but not the time between activities. It can take longer than expected to get children to put their things away, get ready to leave the classroom and then walk down the hall. When children are rushed, everyone's anxiety level goes up (including the teacher's) and children are less cooperative.

Move children gradually. Try to stagger the children's move to the next activity. For example, if you are moving children from group time on the rug to working at their desks, gradually send small groups of children over to begin work. Similarly, if you are moving children from a large group activity to getting ready to go outside, have half the children get their coats while you sing a song, read a book, or play a game with the rest of the children. Then the children can switch places and when everyone has their coats on they can move together to the playground. Make sure that young children do not have time during transitions in which they have nothing to do.

Use imagination. Try gaining children's cooperation and interest during transitions by using imagination and dramatic play. Children are quieter when walking down the hall pretending to be little mice. They will enjoy cleaning up when they pretend to be a big dump truck or a large crane that picks up materials. Children will cooperate better when you wave a magic wand that creates quiet voices or makes everyone tip-toe. Creating a joyful attitude during transitions reduces the tension and helps children feel comfortable.

Keep learning. Engage the children in <u>learning activities</u> to keep them focused during transitions. These activities could be counting by 5 or 10, reciting vocabulary words, practicing phonics rules, singing songs, chanting poems or rhymes, and so on. By giving the children something to focus on, they are less likely to wander or be off task during transitions.

Make special needs adaptations for transitions. Some children with disabilities will need more transitioning time or <u>different procedures</u> than the rest of the class. Children who are highly sensitive to noise and activity may be overwhelmed by the stimuli during transitions. You might want to help the child transition before or after the other children, or to allow the child to wait in a quiet location until the next activity begins. Try visual cues such as reminder cards, photos, and posters and use positive feedback.

Procedures Planning Form

Procedures taught first day:

- ☐ _____
- ☐ _____
- ☐ _____
- ☐ _____
- ☐ _____
- ☐ _____
- ☐ _____

Procedures taught first week:

- ☐ _____
- ☐ _____
- ☐ _____
- ☐ _____
- ☐ _____
- ☐ _____

Other procedures taught during first month:

- ☐ _____
- ☐ _____
- ☐ _____
- ☐ _____
- ☐ _____
- ☐ _____

Get the Children into Routines

This section contains suggestions for some of the more challenging and important procedures. All of these should be taught and practiced during the first few weeks of school. The goal is to get the children to turn these procedures into routines that they can do without thinking much about them.

Lining up and walking in the hallway. Moving the class as a whole group can be intimidating for new teachers and even a challenge for experienced teachers. The trick lies in teaching the procedures for lining up or walking in the hallway clearly. This should be started on the first day of school and repeated as needed afterwards. If children are not behaving properly in the hallways, it is important to stop right away and bring the children back to the room. Keep a positive attitude without making any nasty comments or complaints, and have the children simply practice how to walk in the hallway again. The second important trick is to give positive feedback to the children who are behaving appropriately. Do not spend time trying to correct children. Instead point out who is walking properly or behaving as they should.

Clean up time procedures. In many early childhood classrooms, especially in preschool and kindergarten, clean-up time is the most challenging part of the day for keeping children on-task and reducing inappropriate behaviors. This is not surprising considering the amount of stimulation—noise, movement, materials, and the intensity of the work. There are a few strategies that can ease the difficulty.

- ***Have reasonable goals.*** Throughout the work time/center time period, help children put things away as much as possible so the job at cleanup time is not so difficult. As children finish playing with the dress-up clothes, help them put the materials back. When the block area is overloaded with blocks, you can start to replace some on the shelves. It is often unreasonable to expect that young children can put everything away themselves. It's too big a job.

- ***Be specific.*** Assign very specific and relatively small jobs to children. Asking a child to clean up the block area may be too much, but asking her to put the triangle blocks back on the shelf makes it more doable and more like a game. Similarly, a child can be assigned a puzzle to put away, or to put a few books back on the shelf. This might also help prevent the children from finding other things to begin to play with.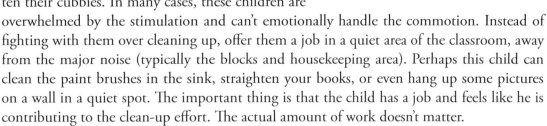

- ***Help overwhelmed children.*** Some children will quickly retreat to a quiet area of the classroom—often their cubbies. In many cases, these children are overwhelmed by the stimulation and can't emotionally handle the commotion. Instead of fighting with them over cleaning up, offer them a job in a quiet area of the classroom, away from the major noise (typically the blocks and housekeeping area). Perhaps this child can clean the paint brushes in the sink, straighten your books, or even hang up some pictures on a wall in a quiet spot. The important thing is that the child has a job and feels like he is contributing to the clean-up effort. The actual amount of work doesn't matter.

Teach children to take care of classroom materials. Like the other procedures we want children to do, taking care of classroom materials <u>needs to be taught</u>. Here are some tips:

- ***Be organized.*** Have a specific place to put things away—markers, books, papers, blocks, etc. Label the area, adding pictures to make it really clear for young children. The more organized you are, the more organized the children will be. This is the critical first step in teaching children to care for classroom materials.

- ***Introduce materials.*** Don't let children use materials until you've introduced the procedures to use them appropriately. Model how you want children to care for the materials, whether it is how to make sure the tops of the markers click when you put them on correctly, or how to turn the pages of the class books so they don't rip. There is almost nothing too simple to model.

- ***Offer reminders.*** Children will need many reminders to learn the proper care of materials. Be supportive by repeating the modeling as needed, or just reiterate things to remember, for example, "As you work on your drawings, remember to put the caps back on the markers and push until they click," or "When you are reading silently, remember how we learned to turn the pages in the books gently."

- ***Give positive feedback.*** Acknowledge when children *do* take care of their things. "Bryan, I noticed you remembered how to turn the pages carefully when you were reading." This way they will begin to pay attention to their own success and know when they are on track. Do this every day.

- ***Use logical consequences.*** If you've followed these steps, and children repeatedly fail to follow your guidelines, then set boundaries by using logical consequences. If a child does not put the caps back on the markers, then she can't use them. If a child doesn't turn the pages of the books gently, he won't be allowed to use them independently. When using logical consequences, your tone of voice must be calm, and the child should always get another chance to use more appropriate behavior soon. If many children are not following the guidelines, then you should go back and have another group lesson on caring for the materials.

Step One Checklist for Teaching Procedures

- ☐ Make a list of all the procedures you want to establish
- ☐ Decide what procedures to teach the first day, first week, first month
- ☐ Plan classroom layout and seating
- ☐ Teach procedures:
    - ☐ Explain the reason
    - ☐ Model the procedure
    - ☐ Children say what they notice
    - ☐ Children practice procedure & get feedback
- ☐ Develop and teach your Quiet Signal
- ☐ Plan and teach procedures for major transitions
- ☐ Teach other procedures gradually over the first month
- ☐ Use positive feedback every few minutes to help children develop appropriate behaviors
- ☐ Create a plan for learning centers
- ☐ Gradually teach procedures to be used at centers

Step 2: Build Classroom Community

Classrooms that have built a good community have strong interpersonal relationships between the teacher and the children and between the children themselves. You might think of building these relationships as making deposits in a social piggy bank (Joseph & Strain, 2006). You will need to make many deposits to build those strong relationships so that children begin to trust you, and so that your relationship stays strong even when you need to set limits.

Many new teachers are warned not to be "friends" with the children. This advice might stem from a fear of losing control or not having enough authority. It is possible and desirable, however, to have a personal relationship with each child that might look like friendship from the outside, but actually represents a caring bond with unconditional positive regard. This must go hand-in-hand with setting limits for children. You can, and should, do both—have a personal relationship with each child, while retaining your authority in order to maintain safety, direct learning, and set limits on behavior.

Help Children Feel They Belong

One of the reasons that teaching is such a hard job is because we are simultaneously planning for the academic learning of a whole community. In some classrooms, the children do not feel part of a community. Instead they may be competitive, highly individualistic, and subgroups may exclude each other or reject certain children from social activities. For example, if your classroom has many instances of tattling, teasing, and bickering, you have a problem with classroom community.

Other classrooms have a deep sense of group cohesion. The children help each other, look out for each other, collaborate and feel a sense of pride in being part of their classroom. This group connection—this sense of a community of learners—happens when the teacher values it and works hard to make it a priority.

An important way to build community in the classroom is through morning meetings. During this meeting, have each child greet each other. This gives children the chance to start the day on a positive note, to learn positive social skills, and to feel welcomed into the group. Pointing out which children are missing that day is a way of showing that you care who comes to school. In the beginning of the school year, carry out a getting-to-know you activity each day. See the ideas below:

Build a Positive Relationship With Children

☐ Greet each child warmly every day.

☐ Ask children about their life outside of school—what they do at home, etc.

☐ Get to know something personal about each child that you can talk about.

☐ Watch children's TV shows and be able to talk to children about the shows.

☐ Let children talk to you about their feelings without being judgmental.

☐ Get to know the children's families. Include multicultural books in your library representing the cultures of your children.

☐ Spend a few minutes as often as you can individually talking to a child.

☐ If you are angry with a child, wash the slate clean at the end of the day and let him or her know you are starting over again fresh the next day.

☐ Let children know they are missed when they are absent.

☐ Put up photos of the children's families.

☐ Provide positive feedback as often as possible throughout the day, aiming for 5 times more positive comments than negative ones.

Use Community Building Activities

Starting the first day of school, plan activities that help the children get to know one another. Here are a few examples:

Classmate scavenger hunt. Make a BINGO game board. In each square put a description that might fit the children in your class, such as "Comes to School on the Bus." Have children talk to each other and try to find a child's name to match each square.

Classroom family book. Children each draw a self portrait, and depending on their age, either dictate or write something about themselves. Laminate or cover the pages in page protectors and put them in a binder that becomes part of the classroom library. Read the book frequently during the beginning of the school year. Here are examples from a first grade classroom unit.

Picture name cards. Take a digital picture of each child and laminate it on a small index card. Punch a hole through the cards and put them on a binder ring. Choose one child to start in the middle of the circle. That child looks at one of the cards, finds that child, says "good morning" and then takes that child's place in the circle. The next child then turns over the next card and starts the process again.

Duck, Duck, Goose name chase. Play by the standard rules for Duck, Duck, Goose, but instead, the child who is "It" says the name of each child (instead of "Duck") as he or she goes around the circle.

Who am I? The children will dictate or write something about themselves privately during the day. Then at group time, you can read each description without telling the name. The children will play a guessing game to figure out who you are describing.

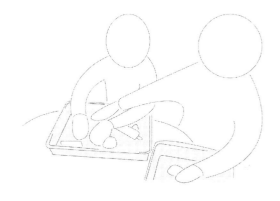

Birthday Messages. For each child's birthday, the class makes a book for the "Birthday Star." The children each make a page that says "_____ is my friend because..." The students draw a picture and write or dictate thoughts about their friend. The birthday child receives a whole book of kind messages. See this story about how well birthday messages work in an inclusion classroom.

Buddy Activities. Pair the children up and have them complete classroom activities together for a week or so. Then mix up the pairs.

Classroom Celebrations. Create a special celebration on a regular basis—such as pajama day or crazy hat day. Have a special snack, read a special book, and sing some songs. Be sure to include everyone in the class celebration. **Never** exclude a child from community-building activities. The children with challenging behavior especially need to feel part of the group.

Classroom Spirit. Choose a name for your classroom community, a class song, class colors, and a mascot. Use these the way sports teams would during your community celebrations and morning meetings. Combine classroom spirit with your classroom celebrations.

Getting to Know You BINGO

B	I	N	G	O
Walks to school	Likes the color blue	Is left handed	Owns a pet	Is wearing sneakers
Likes soccer	Likes to read books	Has brown eyes	Has a younger sibling	Went to the beach this summer
Has a brother	Favorite season is summer	FREE SPACE	Speaks another language besides English	Takes the bus to school
Lives with a grandpartent	Has long hair	Likes to sing	Favorite subject is math	Likes to watch TV
Likes to play video games	Has the same birthday month as me	Ate cereal for breakfast	Likes to go to the movies	Just moved to this area

Classroom Family Book

Name: _____

About Me: _____

_____

_____

_____

_____

Create Classroom Rules

Rules should help children to understand that other people have feelings and that we all have a responsibility for keeping people and things in our classroom safe. For that reason, I recommend only three rules, which focus on 1) how we treat others, 2) how we take care of our things, and 3) how we take care of ourselves. You don't need more rules than these. All other general rules are versions of these three ideas. For example, "Respect others" is a form of "We are kind to others." Most other typical classroom rules, such as "raise your hand" or "listen to the teacher" are actually procedures and should be simply taught through modeling and practice (Step One).

Involve Children in Rule-Making

The process of developing and deciding on these rules can be shared with the children through class meetings. Begin this process by focusing on typical classroom problems: "I noticed that some children were upset today because someone was calling them names. What do you think we can do about this problem?" By focusing on specific problems in the classroom, you can help children under-

stand the reason for rules. It is very important for children's moral development that they understand these reasons rather than follow the rules because of fear of getting in trouble. You can repeatedly emphasize why rules are important and how they help keep us all safe and keep the classroom in good shape.

You may find that you will need to divide each rule into simpler, more specific behaviors. For example, children may want to create a rule, "We don't call each other names." It is especially effective when the children themselves have developed such a rule. Remember, however, to keep your discussion of rules focused on behaviors that are true all the time—otherwise you may be describing procedures, which are much simpler to just teach children through modeling and repeated practice. In essence, rules are about living as a community and maintaining good relationships with each other. Procedures are about how to get specific things done. The difference is important in how we help children develop moral reasoning and an understanding of living in a classroom community (DeVries & Zan, 1994).

Special Tip:

Simply posting rules on the wall doesn't mean children will follow them. You must constantly model good behavior and help children learn how to behave kindly, to take care of their things, and to be safe.

Classroom Rules:

We are kind to others.

We stay safe and take care of ourselves.

We take care of our materials and classroom.

Help Children to Live by Classroom Rules

Children will naturally test the limits on what they are allowed to say and do. This includes bullying, saying disparaging things to other children, and rejecting classmates. In order to create a healthy classroom community, it is critical to stop these behaviors immediately. If you let even the smallest negative comment go unchallenged, you will give the message to the children that being nasty to others is acceptable. It's not.

For example, you might overhear children saying things like:

"You can't come to my birthday."

"She smells bad."

"Look at what she's wearing!"

"Oooh, that's for girls!"

"You can't play with us."

"You're stupid."

"I don't like you."

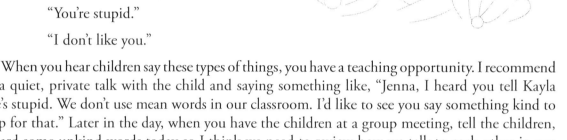

When you hear children say these types of things, you have a teaching opportunity. I recommend having a quiet, private talk with the child and saying something like, "Jenna, I heard you tell Kayla that she's stupid. We don't use mean words in our classroom. I'd like to see you say something kind to make up for that." Later in the day, when you have the children at a group meeting, tell the children, "I've heard some unkind words today so I think we need to review how we talk to each other in our classroom." Then you can review your poster with kind words, and talk about how it feels when others say mean things to us.

After a few instances of this type of discussion, the children will realize that they are psychologically safe in your classroom. This will help stop the type of behavior that leads to bullying, because children will not have to constantly worry about other people being unkind.

Use Positive Teacher Responses

The most powerful tool you have for creating a positive community is the way you talk to the children. Lots of positive comments and responses build positive energy. It's also important to monitor other types of language that are more harmful.

- ***Positive feedback.*** "I see three children have their books out and open." "Marcia and Judy, you shared your materials well today." "You mixed red and blue in your painting. How did you make these lines?" Often called <u>narrating the positive,</u> this is encouraging talk that describes the positive things your children are doing, whether it is good behaviors or academics. It shows that you are interested in their work and efforts. This language is effective because it provides clear feedback to the children about what they are doing right.

- *Empty praise.* Short comments like "good job" and "nice work" feel good and help create a positive environment, however children don't learn much from them about why they did a good job, or what aspect of their work is good. These comments are like junk food. They taste good, but are not very nutritious.

- *Manipulative praise.* "I like the way Kody is cleaning up." Children quickly learn that these statements are coercive and are not sincere. They pit one child against the others and can lead to resentment. Instead, try describing what children are doing that is appropriate in an anonymous way: "Some children are ready, sitting quietly on the rug with legs crossed." This will probably take some practice to get used to but it's worth the effort.

- *Negative nagging.* "Jared, stop that." "No calling out." "You were all very noisy in the hall." "Shhh!" These statements draw attention to the behaviors you don't want to occur. Instead, use positive feedback to focus the children's attention on what your expectations are. If a child needs correction, it should be done privately.

- *Humiliation.* "You'll never make it to 3rd grade if you keep that up." "Who do you think you are?" "What's wrong with you?" These statements are never appropriate and come from extreme frustration—a sign that a teacher needs extra support to turn things around and plenty of work on her own emotional regulation. Needless to say, these comments encourage children to become defensive and act out, or humiliated and shut down. They also teach the children that it's acceptable to use humiliating language and to bully each other.

Teacher Language

Positive Feedback — Healthy ☺

Empty Praise

Manipulative Praise

Negative Nagging

Humiliation ☹ — Unhealthy

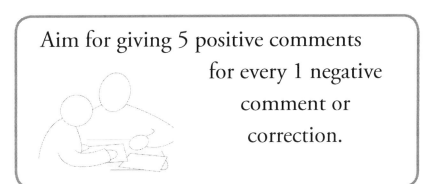

Aim for giving 5 positive comments for every 1 negative comment or correction.

Step 2 Checklist for Building a Community of Learners

☐ Develop a positive relationship with each child in your class

☐ Plan activities to help the children get to know each other

☐ Create classroom rules with the children's input

☐ Remind children of the rules and review them frequently

☐ Give positive comments frequently—5 times as many as negative ones

☐ Provide positive feedback to help children learn appropriate behaviors

Step 3: Teach Classroom Success Skills

Being successful as a student requires more than being smart. It demands a whole set of skills for surviving and flourishing in a classroom. In order to succeed children need to be able to:

- Listen to the teacher and do what is asked
- Control their impulses (stop doing what they want to do, or when they want to do it)
- Tolerate frustration (when they don't get what you want, or have to stop)
- Focus on one task and ignore distractions
- Ask appropriately for what they want or need
- Get attention in appropriate ways
- Initiate friendships
- Make amends when they do something wrong
- Say "no" or "stop" in appropriate ways

There are many more skills we could add to this list, of course. Children who do not yet know how to do these things often end up using inappropriate behavior like grabbing, ignoring requests, distracting others, fighting, or daydreaming. Teaching these skills on a regular basis can prevent challenging behaviors and create a positive, harmonious classroom.

You might be thinking that there is already so much to be taught in your over-packed curriculum that you couldn't possibly devote critical class time to these social and emotional skills. Don't overlook the importance of this step because it can make the difference as to whether you are exhausted at the end of the day, or satisfied by your teaching. Behavior problems can slow down the progress of the entire class as you waste time dealing with children who are off task, hurting each other, or who have shut down emotionally and can't learn.

Teach Children to Regulate their Behavior

Many behavior problems are the result of children's difficulty with self-regulation. Because children learn self-regulation better when it is embedded throughout the day, rather than as separate teaching activities, you can integrate the following self-regulation strategies into your classroom management plans (Bodrova & Leong, 2007):

Freeze games. Include games in which children must listen and regulate their bodies' actions within a fun framework. You can ask a question, put on music, and when the music stops, ask the children to freeze, then respond. *Hopscotch*, *Mother May I* and *Simon Says* are other games that help children regulate their physical behavior.

Stillness time. Build into your schedule a meditation or relaxation time in which all the children sit quietly for a couple of minutes. Teach them to sit comfortably with their eyes closed. Ring a bell or other sound to get started, then guide the children in listening to the sounds in the room, or paying attention to how their body is sitting. Start with just a minute at first, then gradually build up to three or four. This will be challenging for some children in the beginning, but if you practice it every day, you'll be amazed at how quickly children can learn to control their bodies.

Picture and symbols. Use pictures and symbols of what behavior children should be doing to help learn self-discipline until they can do it independently. For example, when children are sharing with each other in pairs, one child can hold a stick with a picture of an ear on it (for the listener) and the other child can hold a stick with a picture of a mouth on it (for the speaker). A photo of how a child should be sitting can be laminated and held in the child's hand during group time. Other mediators include picture cards to help children remember rules and directions, graphics of the daily schedule for children to refer to, squares on the carpet to designate personal space, and written learning plans.

Self-monitoring charts. Often children do not even realize when they are off-task, bothering others, or behaving in inappropriate ways. Having a concrete way for them to keep track of how well they are doing can be very effective. The first step is to figure out two or three behaviors that you'll focus on. This should be done with the child helping to choose so that he is invested in the task. Say something like, "I have a great way for you to learn new ways to behave. You'll be like the boss who keeps track of yourself and decides how you're doing each day. Let me explain it to you. First we need to figure out what you want to learn how to do better. I think we should focus on when you first come into the classroom in the morning. What could you do better?" Hopefully the child will be able to identify a few behaviors, with your guidance. Next, make a chart that will help him to keep track of the new behavior. Be sure to have *the child* mark the chart; don't do it yourself or it won't teach self-regulation. Review the chart each day and offer encouragement. No punishment should happen if a child doesn't reach his goal. Instead, help him to practice the skills she needs to be successful.

Self-Monitoring Chart

Behavior	Monday	Tuesday	Wednesday	Thursday	Friday
	😊 😐 ☹️	😊 😐 ☹️	😊 😐 ☹️	😊 😐 ☹️	😊 😐 ☹️
	😊 😐 ☹️	😊 😐 ☹️	😊 😐 ☹️	😊 😐 ☹️	😊 😐 ☹️
	😊 😐 ☹️	😊 😐 ☹️	😊 😐 ☹️	😊 😐 ☹️	😊 😐 ☹️
	😊 😐 ☹️	😊 😐 ☹️	😊 😐 ☹️	😊 😐 ☹️	😊 😐 ☹️

Teach Children to Control Emotions

Children need to learn to calm down when they are upset and to tolerate frustration when things don't go their way. In order to use these skills, children need to be aware of and identify their own emotions.

Identify and label feelings. Often children exhibit challenging behaviors because they are unable to understand or cope with their own feelings or understand others'. The first step for teachers is to help children recognize how emotions are expressed. This can be done directly through picture cards that you might hold up and have the children discuss, or by reading children's literature related to emotional expression, such as:

- *Glad Monster, Sad Monster: A Book About Emotions* (Emberley & Miranda, 1997) is a charming book for preschoolers with masks children can try on. Feelings are represented as different colors.

- *Alexander and the Terrible, Horrible, No Good, Very Bad Day* (Viorst, 2009) offers primary grade children the opportunity to discuss themes of dealing with frustration and anger management.

- *The Rainbow Fish* (Pfister, 1992) provides a situation for discussing how it feels to be rejected by peers and the importance of friendship. Appropriate for preschool through primary grades, the book is beautifully illustrated and appealing to children.

- *Today I Feel Silly: And Other Moods That Make My Day* (Curtis, 1998) reviews various different moods that will help preschoolers through primary grade children reflect on their own changes in mood.

- *Let's Talk About Feeling Sad* (Berry, 1996) is one of a series of books appropriate for preschool and kindergarten about specific feelings. Other books in this series include feeling afraid, embarrassed, angry, disappointed, and jealous.

There are also a variety of children's books available for bibliotherapy which help children cope with behavioral and emotional challenges by relating to the stories in the books, or helping them to discuss difficult subjects such as divorce, death, adoption, bullying, self-esteem, worrying, and many other emotional and social topics (Abdullah, 2002; Sridhar & Vaughn, 2000). These can be found through an Internet search or by asking your school or local librarian for recommendations.

Display emotion photos. You might consider taking photographs of the children to hang on the wall with the emotions labeled. You can refer to these when children are expressing emotions and scaffold the children's use of these pictures and labels in their writing, discussions and interactions.

Use an emotion thermometer. Create a thermometer that shows different moods. As children relax they can use the thermometer as a concrete way of showing their emotional intensity. This can also be helpful in getting children to express their emotions.

Acknowledge and accept feelings. Help children learn that feelings and actions are separate things. For example, we might feel angry but it is our choice how to express our anger. We should never criticize or demean children for their feelings, or else they will learn that their feelings don't matter or that they are not really feeling what they think they are feeling. Instead, say something like, "Shelly, you seem very frustrated, but I can't let you hurt anyone. Let's go to the Quiet Corner for a little while."

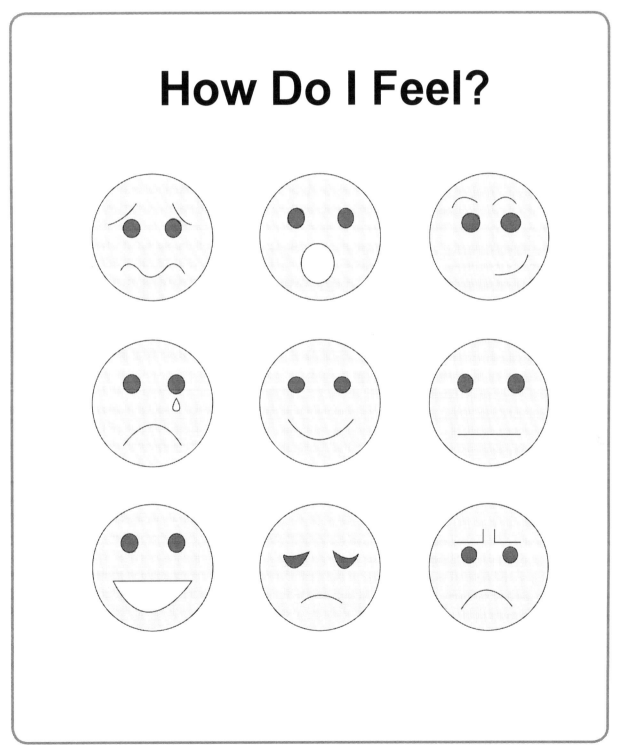

Teach Children to Calm Down

The following section provides <u>practical ways</u> of teaching children to calm themselves down. The only way these exercises work, however, is if they are regularly practiced when the children are calm. These skills must be learned ***before*** they are needed. Pick a few of these that you like and try to fit them into your daily routine so that it is easy to remember to practice them.

Breathing exercises

Controlling your breath is the easiest and most effective way to calm down. These activities can be taught to the entire class and then brief reminders should be used to give individual support when needed.

- ☐ ***Flower and candle.*** The children hold up their fists and pretend they are flowers. They deeply smell the pretend flower. With the other hand, they pretend their fists are candles. After smelling the flower, they slowly blow out the candles. Be sure to remind them to blow out the candle gently so that they slow down their respiration.

- ☐ ***Three in and three out.*** Get the children in a relaxed position, then have them close their eyes and breathe in as you count "one." Then, without breathing out, have them breathe in a bit deeper as you count to "two," then once more have them fully fill their lungs as you count "three." The exhale works the same way. You say, "Okay, one, now exhale a little bit," Next you say, "Two, blow out a little more," and then, "Three, let out the rest of your breath." This works best if you model this first a few times and have them do it with you before starting to close their eyes. They can also pretend to gradually blow up a balloon with each breath and then let the air out slowly.

- ☐ ***Blowing bubbles.*** Have children practice gently blowing through the wand to create bubbles. Encourage children to make different size bubbles and to slow down. Have the children watch them drift away until it pops before blowing the next bubble.

- ☐ ***Snow globe.*** Shake up a snow globe and ask the child to watch the glitter slowly settle, breathing along with the movement.

Body grounding

Grounding exercises focus on using the child's body to help him or her stay in the present moment and not get caught up in worries about the past or future. They are particularly helpful when the child is over-stimulated or needs to calm down and with children who are chronically anxious, have experienced trauma, or have unstable lives.

- ☐ ***Tighten and release.*** While the children are sitting down, have them tighten their fists and count to three slowly and then completely relax their fists, and count to three slowly. Repeat this three or four times at the beginning of activities to get children to calm their bodies and get ready for more focused work. Children can also be taught to use this technique before taking any action when they are angry.

- ☐ *Growing roots.* Have the children sit in a chair and place their feet flat on the floor and really feel the solid weight of their feet connecting to the floor. Then have them imagine that they are a plant with roots which are growing deep into the ground to keep them safe and solid, so they won't be blown around by worries.

- ☐ *Cool down.* Have the child get a damp paper towel to hold on his forehead that will take away the worries/anger/frustration/sadness. Encourage the child to sit in a quiet spot for a few moments and feel the coolness. Let him decide when he is ready to rejoin the activities.

- ☐ *Special calming objects.* Children can choose a small object, such as a stone, piece of cloth, or something with an interesting texture since the sensory effects are helpful. When children are upset, they can reach into their pocket, cubby, or desk and spend a couple of minutes feeling these objects.

- ☐ *Peaceful colors.* Gather the children together in a comfortable spot and have them close their eyes and pick a color that makes them feel quiet and calm and peaceful. Then have them imagine that with each breath they take the peaceful color spreads all over their body, calming each place it goes—for example, down their neck to their chest, then their stomach, arms, legs, and so on until they are filled with beautiful color and peaceful feelings.

- ☐ *Soothing music.* In your Quiet Corner you can have soothing music and headphones for when children need some peace and quiet. You can make these available during free times during the day, center time, or you can suggest that children might want to use them when they are showing signs of agitation.

Yoga Poses

Yoga can help children gain body awareness and self-control of their bodies, which is an important step in self-regulation. The following are some possible poses to use with young children. Have the children pay attention to their breathing while in the poses. Have fun with these and encourage children to create their own poses, too!

- ☐ **Mountain.** This is a good pose to start with. Show the children a picture of a mountain and have them imagine how straight, tall and steady they can be while standing still. Hold shoulders slightly back and feet flat on the floor.

- ☐ *Cat/Dog.* Children get down on hands and knees. Arms should be right under the shoulders with their back flat. They gently arch their back up high like a cat as they breath out. Then as they breath in, they let their back sag down like a dog. Gently alternate between the two for a few more breaths.

- ☐ *Tree.* Children stand on one leg with the opposite foot resting against their ankle or calf. After they've gained your balance, they gently raise their arms like a tree as they exhale. Hold the "branches" up in the air for a few more breaths.

- ☐ *Happy baby.* Children lay on their back and grab the soles of their feet in the air. Gently rocking back and forth provides a back massage and loosens tight muscles.
- ☐ *Cobra.* Children lay on their stomach and push up with their arms, arching their back.

Calming Thoughts

In addition to using the body to calm down, children can also learn to use thoughts to calm themselves down or to feel better when they are frightened, sad, or angry. Practice this frequently.

- ☐ **Describe the room.** Have the children look around the room and begin to describe it out loud. "I see a table with books on it. There is a pencil next to the books. Under the table, the floor is grey with lines in it." You can model this and have children take turns practicing it. When needed, remind children they can play the "room game" to calm down.
- ☐ **ABC's.** Teach the children to use the alphabet as a calming routine. They can quietly whisper the letters to themselves. Have them go through the alphabet once, then repeat it a second time, stretching out the sound of each letter.
- ☐ **Kind thoughts.** Help the children make a list of kind things they could say to themselves such as "I am a good person," "I am loved," or "I can do this." Help the children practice saying these phrases to themselves, perhaps in a whisper. Older children may be able to hear these thoughts internally, but younger children will do better with moving their lips.
- ☐ **Favorites.** The children can practice thinking about their favorite things. It might be helpful to offer categories such as favorite foods, people, toys, pets, places to go, friends, etc. Once again, remind children to mentally list their favorite things when they need to calm down.
- ☐ **Friendly photos.** Ask families to send in photos of people who are important to their child. Laminate these and attach them with a small-ring binder or twist-tie. When children are feeling sad/angry/lonely they can pull out their photos for a moment or two and let the photos sooth them.
- ☐ **Visual imagery.** Have the children close their eyes and imagine themselves in a calm, happy place where they feel warm and safe. Tell them that they can go back to this place and feel good by closing their eyes and bringing this image into their mind. As children get tired or cranky throughout the day, you can remind them to close their eyes for a moment and go back to their happy place. This can also be done to quiet the entire class before beginning a new activity.
- ☐ **Self-talk.** Help children to control their emotional responses by having them repeat words quietly out loud. These words might be, "I am calm," "Stop and think," "I can wait, I can wait," or "I can do this!". This can be learned as a game. You can put on lively music and have the children dance vigorously, then stop the music and have them say in a quiet voice "I am calm." Children can also create cards with phrases on them for reminders. When children show signs of agitation, they can be reminded to use self-talk by you modeling it.

Self-Talk Cards

I can wait.

I am calm.

Stop and think!

I can do this.

Turtle Technique

<u>This strategy</u> involves teaching children to have self-control by pretending to be a turtle when they are upset or angry (Center for Social and Emotional Foundations of Learning, n.d.; C. Webster-Stratton, 1991). They go into their "shell," count to three, and then think of a better solution. Click <u>here</u> for a PowerPoint file to print out and make into a book. Here are the steps:

1. Model remaining calm
2. Teach the child the steps of how to control feelings and calm down ("Think like a turtle")

    Step 1: Recognize your feeling(s)

    Step 2: Think "Stop"

    Step 3: Tuck inside your "shell" and take three deep breaths

    Step 4: Come out when calm and think of a "solution"

3. Practice these steps frequently
4. Prepare for and help the child handle possible disappointment or change and "to think of a solution"

Possible solutions:
   a. Get a teacher
   b. Ask nicely
   c. Say, "Please"
   d. Ignore
   e. Share
   f. Say, "Please stop"
   g. Trade a toy/item
   h. Wait and take turns

5. Give positive feedback and attention when the child stays calm
6. Teach families the "Turtle Technique" to use at home

Teach Academic Survival Skills

Some children use inappropriate behavior because they have not learned how to behave in school. You might have a tendency to think children are just "acting out," but they may need support in learning how to get their work done and to sustain their attention. These skills include:

- ☐ Getting started on independent work
- ☐ Looking at the teacher while she is talking or leading a lesson
- ☐ Taking a short break and getting back to work
- ☐ Asking for help

☐ Raising one's hand and waiting to respond

☐ Following what the teacher asks

☐ Organizing one's books and materials

☐ Nodding to show understanding

☐ Asking the teacher to give feedback

These skills are often overlooked because many children learn them without extra help. But other children need direct instruction. I've found that teachers are often angry and frustrated with children who lack these skills—and make the assumption that the children just choose not to use them. Children with disabilities are particularly likely to need support for developing academic survival skills, especially in inclusion settings.

Try out a simple skills training program. Pick one or two skills from the list above. Designate some time during the school day to model and support the child in practicing the new skill. Give positive feedback when the child is successful. Practice this over the course of at least a few weeks, because it takes time for children to develop new skills to the point where they can use them on their own.

Teach Children to Get Positive Attention

What's the difference between the children who are a joy to have in class and the children who push our buttons and challenge our last bit of patience? One important difference is that some children have learned how to get adults' attention in positive ways and others haven't. Consider the subtle ways that children interact positively with you:

☐ Saying, "Good morning, Ms. Jones!"

☐ Bringing you pictures they've drawn

☐ Giving you a hug

☐ Saying, "You're the best teacher in the world!"

☐ Making eye contact and smiling

☐ Asking you about your personal life: "What's your dog's name?"

These interactions represent a way of building personal relationships that we as adults also use in everyday life. You can think of these interactions as the grease for the wheels of relationship-building. And without that grease, the wheels turn slowly, squeak, grind, and wear down.

The good news is that you can teach children how to get attention in positive ways. Model positive things they can say to you and other adults, and have them practice. Use puppets with younger children or personal lists of things to say written on index cards for older children. Suggest to the child that he can shake your hand when he comes into the classroom, or ask how you are feeling. When the child begins to use any of these strategies, give plenty of positive attention and feedback. As children begin to get more attention in positive ways, they will have less of a need to get this attention by using inappropriate behavior. Helping children learn these new strategies takes a while, so be patient.

Teach Children to Pay Attention and Focus

An important thing to remember is that children need to be taught how to pay attention and focus. The more we model and help children practice these skills, the better they will learn.

Tracking. Teach children to keep their eyes on the person who is talking. This is a simple skill, but many distracted children don't practice it! Remind the children to look at you or other children who are talking. They should also turn their body to face the speaker.

Take a break and return. During independent work, all of us take frequent breaks from concentration, even if we don't notice it (how often have you checked Pinterest lately?) Teach children to take quick breaks, such as looking out the window, stretching their arms or legs, or closing their eyes for a moment. Then teach them to get right back to what they were doing. Visual aids can help. Tape a picture of a child working (either listening to the teacher or working on their seatwork) and write: "Am I Focused?" on it as a reminder. Here's an example:

Another way to make this skill more concrete is to have a child use an individual timer at his desk. Set the time for 30 seconds or one minute, let the child get up, move around, get a drink of water, and so on. When the timer goes off, he needs to start his work again right away.

Fidget toys. It sounds counter-intuitive but some children respond very well to a small toy that they can "fidget" with. These can help the child find something to do with his or her hands instead of bothering others or finding something to play with. They also help children who daydream and zone out. Try using a kush ball, a pipe cleaner, squeeze ball, or a ball of playdo.

Teaching Peer Relationship Skills

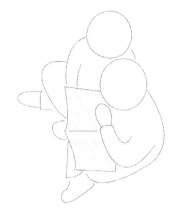

Social skills are critical for children's success in school. Many times children use inappropriate behavior like poking, hitting, or biting because they have not learned how to get other children's attention or manage social demands. In addition, children who are rejected or lack friends can be very uncomfortable. This social anxiety prevents them from using the part of their brains they need for learning. Children's books are a terrific way to helping learn social skills. Here are some other ideas:

Support the development of friendships. Some children will easily develop positive relationships with other children. Some will not and will need more direct instruction, modeling, and support from you and the environment. Provide consistent time in the daily routine for shared activities. For preschool and kindergarten, this should be an extended time for children to play and use learning centers with other children. For elementary grades, include a regular learning center time in which children can work in pairs or small groups, collaborative activities in which children work together towards a single goal or product, and buddy activities such as *Think-Pair-Share*.

Help aggressive or withdrawn children. We might be tempted to conclude that some children are aggressive or shy and we need to live with it. Not so. Children need help in learning social strategies and will benefit from your careful observations and modeling. For example, if you were working with a preschool boy who has difficulty getting the group in the block area to accept him in their play, you might join the play with him, modeling strategies: "Look kids, Kenny has some flat blocks that would be great for ramps. Where do you think he should put them?" Encourage Kenny to be persistent in his attempts. Puppets can be effective with preschool and kindergarten children in modeling skills.

Working with elementary children requires more subtlety and sometimes more direct coaching. If necessary, teach children to make eye contact and smile. Try to convince them of the importance of being positive. Children who are angry and negative have more difficulty making friends. You can set up role plays where children practice saying positive things to each other. There are a variety of published social-skills training programs available. Check with your school social worker or counselor for suggestions.

To help with shyness, be sure to set up a variety of activities that can be done in pairs. For children who have not yet mastered social skills, having to coordinate a relationship with more than one other person can be overwhelming. Encourage parents to make play dates with another child by suggesting children who might be good playmates.

Help Rejected Children. Some children will be left out frequently, either because of withdrawal or excessive aggressiveness. What might happen is that such children begin to be seen by the other children in a role—for example, the kid who's always in trouble, or the class clown, or the quiet kid. Help children get un-stuck from such roles by allowing the child (and the other children) to see themselves in a different light. For example, imagine that 1st grader Kendra has little impulse control and is often bossy. She occasionally hits the other children and they have learned to avoid her. You can turn this around by pointing out whenever you catch Kendra doing anything kind. For example one of the children might have dropped a book that Kendra picks up. You can say, "Kendra, thanks for picking up that book for Michael. *You're such a good friend.*" When Kendra and the other children hear this enough, it will start to become a self-fulfilling prophesy.

Outside recreational time is also an important setting for social skills development. Children act differently when they don't have the structure of the indoor classroom and friendships often bloom in this setting. Unfortunately, often times in kindergarten and elementary grades, outside time is limited to short periods of recess. Recess time is sometimes stressful, especially in urban areas in which children have few activities available, overcrowding, and less-than-perfect supervision. Too often children return from recess over-stimulated and distressed. In such settings, consider getting permission to take the children on neighborhood walks or to parks.

Teach Children to Say Kind Words

It is an unfortunate truth that some children do not hear many kind words and they need those models desperately. All young children can benefit from direct instruction in how to use kind words. Young children are still learning about what the boundaries are for their behavior, and they need us to be clear about what is okay to say in school and what is not. At group time, you can begin by using puppets, dolls, or pictures of children and put on a little skit in which you act out a child saying mean words. Ask the children how they would feel if they heard those words. Next ask them what we can say to each other to make each other feel good, instead of sad or angry. Make a list of the words on chart paper and post it in a place the children can see.

For the next few days, at the start of group time, re-read the chart of kind words. When you hear children using kind words, draw attention to it. At the end of the day, gather the children together and share the kind words you heard that day. Add any new ones to your list. You should see a great decrease in teasing as you focus children on kindness instead.

Even after the first week of this practice, you will still need periodic reminders. Choose one day each week to go over the Kind Words list and continue to provide positive attention and feedback when you hear children using them. After the children have gotten good at this, you can use the same method to teach them how to do kind things for each other. Start by having the children brainstorm a list of kind things they can do. Put these on a large poster and hang it where you and the children can refer to it frequently. Then have the children act out scenes in which they do kind acts as practice.

Kind Words:

I like your picture!

Can I help you?

Great job!

Thank you

Please

Want to play?

Thanks for your help!

You look nice

I'm sorry

Excuse me

Do you want some, too?

Are you okay?

Good answer!

School Success Skills Training Worksheet

Skill to be Taught	When in Daily Schedule the Skill Will Be Practiced	Children Who Need Extra Practice

Step 3 Checklist for Teaching Classroom Success Skills

Behavioral Regulation throughout the Day:
- ☐ Have children plan activities
- ☐ Play freeze games
- ☐ Institute a "Stillness Time"
- ☐ Use pictures and symbols to teach behaviors
- ☐ Create self-monitoring charts

Emotional Regulation:
- ☐ Identify and label feelings
- ☐ Acknowledge and accept feelings
- ☐ Teach children to calm down
- ☐ Teach breathing exercises
- ☐ Use body grounding
- ☐ Incorporate Yoga poses
- ☐ Teach calming thoughts

Academic Survival Skills:
- ☐ Teach children to get positive attention
- ☐ Teach children how to pay attention and focus

Peer Relationship Skills:
- ☐ Support the development of friendships
- ☐ Plan collaborative activities
- ☐ Teach social relationship skills
- ☐ Teach kind words

Step 4: Engage Children in Learning

At the heart of classroom management is the ability to keep the children engaged in learning. Many behavior problems result when children are not actively participating in the learning activities. This is often because the work is too easy or too hard but it might also be due to the choice of procedures that you use when conducting lessons or activities. Deciding what format to use to carry out a lesson or activity is important in engaging children effectively. Many teachers find themselves with behavior problems and management headaches because they have chosen a format that is not best-suited to the type of activity or to the age of their children. Once you've chosen a format, be sure you are using it effectively as described in the rest of this step.

Make Whole-Group Lessons Effective

Whole-group activities are effective only when all the children are able to participate. When children have to wait for a turn to participate, or listen at length to other children talk, they will quickly lose interest and may become disruptive. Whole-group settings are not appropriate when many sets of materials are needed. Conducting an experiment and having children watch you rather than use the materials themselves is not effective. Instead, plan these hands-on activities for smaller groups, or learning centers.

It is not always effective to use whole-group settings for teaching concepts in literacy or math when the children are not all at the same level of understanding or readiness. You may be engaging the middle level of the group, but there may be children who already know the material and are not interested, or children who are not ready to learn the new material. These children may tune out and find something more interesting which results in your need to constantly redirect them.

> *Special Tip:*
> If you find that you are using a lot of energy to keep the children's attention, consider using learning centers, work stations, or small–group structures instead.

Keep it short. Brain research (and careful observation) shows that children cannot sustain their attention in a whole group lesson for long and will not be able to learn the information after they lose focus. As a rule of thumb, consider the age of the children as a g*u*ide to how many minutes for your lessons. Multiple mini-lessons throughout the day are more effective than longer whole group lessons. Brain breaks, such as moving around the room, stretching or running, can help children get ready to focus again.

Use good questions. Questions can provide important scaffolding for children's emerging understanding of concepts and they can help you assess children's comprehension. The way you use questioning, however, can result in active engagement or, unfortunately, unengaged and disruptive children. Try these strategies:

1. Plan out your questions ahead of time. Write them down and have them nearby to refer to if necessary.

2. Use all levels of Bloom's taxonomy in developing your questions so they encourage critical thinking rather than just spitting back what they remember.

3. To encourage critical thinking, ask children to explain the processes they used.

4. Know what a good answer would be so you can extend children's responses.

Provide think time. Most teachers wait less than a second before expecting an answer to a question. You might say, "Keep your hands down and take a minute to think of this question and then I'll ask you to share. After several seconds (or more) you can begin to ask children to share. In preschool you might want to ask the children to close their eyes and think of an answer for a moment or two before responding. Children will provide more thoughtful answers when they have time to think.

Don't overdo it. Asking too many questions is not productive. Children will quickly lose interest in what other children are saying, so keep the pace fairly quick and use questions sparingly. Encourage children to ask their *own* questions of each other or of you. For example, after reading an informational text, you might say to the children, "What questions do you have about the book?"

Use Alternatives to Hand Raising

A teacher asks a question and waits for the hands to go up. Many do, some waving wildly. Many don't, the children staring into space or playing with the rug. Some children seem to still call out, no matter the grade level. Often the child doesn't know the answer and stumbles for a minute or so before the teacher moves onto to someone else. Sometimes the child does answer in a correct, thoughtful way, while the rest of the children zone out or anxiously wait for their own turn. The teacher is often exhausted from trying to keep the children on task.

Sound familiar? Young children don't learn well from sitting and listening to others, even if they can get themselves to be able to focus on the interaction. This is an ineffective learning pattern, yet teachers repeat it because it's so familiar and comfortable. Here are better alternatives:

Turn and Talk. After the question is asked, pairs of children turn to each other. One listens while the other answers. This way half of the class is engaged in talking, and it is easier for children to pay attention to the speaker in a paired situation. Be sure that children know ahead of time who their partner is and that they practice how to pair up. This should move quickly, so keep the pace brisk.

Think-Pair-Share. This technique is similar to Turn and Talk, except that children are first given time to solve a problem or answer a question individually, then they turn to their partner, quickly share responses with each other and come up with the best or most interesting answer. Next the teacher calls on a few pairs to share with the class. Being able to listen to a partner is a challenge for young children, but the practice they get will help them develop more self-regulation.

Choral responses. To increase student engagement and reinforce simple concepts, allow the children to respond all together. This works best for questions with one answer, and as a quick review of previously covered material.

Individual whiteboards. Each child has a whiteboard and marker and they write down their answer to the question. Children hold up their boards so the teacher can judge how well the children are understanding the concepts.

Cold call. Keep a list of children's names, put their names on cards, or sticks, and randomly pick children's names to answer. This helps to improve the pace of the lesson, and keeps children engaged and ready to answer since they don't know when they will be called on. It also ensures that all children get a chance to participate and a few children are not dominating the discussions. Keep it positive. This should not be humiliating or embarrassing. Make sure that the children are able to be successful with the content you are reviewing.

> ***Special Tip:***
> Post the following chart on your wall to help you remember alternatives to the ineffective hand-rasing routine.

Alternatives to Hand Raising

1. Turn and Talk

2. Think-Pair-Share

3. Choral Responses

4. Individual Whiteboards

5. Cold Calling

Make Seatwork Successful

When you give assignments for children to work on independently at their seats, two strategies are important. First, be sure that you have given children enough preparation so that they can work on their own and not need you to repeat the instructions. At the beginning of the seatwork period, be sure that the children have really engaged in the work. Second, you should circulate around the room, giving help individually where it is needed, but keeping your discussion brief and private so as not to interfere with the other children's work.

Plan for when children are done early. Be sure to plan something interesting for children to do if they are ready for the next activity before the other children are. When children have nothing specific to do, they will find something to engage themselves and this may not be what you want them to be doing. Some teachers use Choice Boards with activities listed on them to allow the children to choose an activity when they are done. I've also seen Task Cards and buckets with activities, and packets that children keep in their desk.

Stop the chatting during seatwork. Many teachers struggle with children talking during seatwork. Review with the children how to work independently and what to do if they have a question. Give lots of positive feedback during seatwork, pointing out who is working appropriately. Make sure that your physical environment supports the behavior you expect. For example, many teachers group children at tables, or push desks together in clusters. This is very conducive to cooperative small group activities, but can be problematic during seatwork. Research suggests that involvement and efficiency during seatwork is higher when children are in structured rows rather than clusters, especially for children with behavioral or learning challenges (Bennett, 1983).

Give good directions. If you are giving directions to the whole class, use your quiet signal first and be sure that you have the children's attention. Only give one or two directions at a time. This is especially helpful for English language learners. Only give directions that are necessary in that moment, and give them in a way that tells the child specifically what to do. Be clear and concrete; telling a child to "settle down" or to "get ready" does not state what behaviors the child should follow. Instead, say, "Sit back in your seat and use your whisper voice," or "Take your journal out and put your pencil next to it." This lets the children know exactly what they should do. Give the children time to respond to your request before making another one. Monitor the children to be sure they follow your directions.

Some children, especially those with disabilities, may need personalized directions. They might respond better when you give them a physical prompt (pointing, guiding, demonstrating). It is helpful to also have picture prompts for directions that are given often, such as washing hands, hanging up coats, getting books out for lessons, or pushing in chairs. For children with verbal processing problems, pictures can help them manage the complex verbal environment of the classroom.

Make Sharing Time and Group Discussions Effective

Another common form of group activity is one in which each child takes the floor and provides a narrative about something he experienced outside of school, often with a concrete object to go along with the talk. Similarly, many teachers build in these types of group discussions after reading a book to the class and have the children take turns describing their personal responses.

These types of discussions are difficult to manage in any classroom, and there are added challenges when working with young children. In order to participate in discussions, children must learn to take turns speaking, and you will need to decide how those turns will be managed. Will you call on children who raise their hands? Call on children in order so everyone gets a turn? Go around the circle? Next, children will need to speak relevantly on the topic. It takes practice and skill for you to redirect children or ensure that the rest of the group doesn't become restless and lose interest in the speaker. Given the complexity and difficulty in leading discussions with young children, there are some adaptations that will help things go more smoothly:

- Keep discussions short (5 to 10 minutes) and use them sparingly. Don't have all the children take turns sharing at one meeting. Break it up over a few days with a few children at a time.

- Use visual aids to help children keep their attention and focus. If you are discussing the best part of a book, show that picture. If children are sharing what they did, encourage them to create a picture or dramatize what happened with the help of friends.

- Teach the children to keep their eyes on the speaker. This will help them focus better.

- Redirect children as needed. It may feel rude to interrupt children, but you are also serving as a guide to help them realize when they are not holding the interest of the group. This can be done gently: "Marisa, what a wonderful story. We need to move on to the next child, though, so I hope you will tell me the rest of your adventures later during center time."

- Try to engage all the children as much as possible. Encourage the group to ask questions or to comment on what the speaker is saying in order to help them stay focused and interested.

- Remember the children's developmental levels. What might seem like misbehavior will often be immaturity and inability to sustain focus in discussion settings. Watch the children's body language carefully. When they are fidgety and restless, try to speed up the pace, or cut the discussion short and move onto a different activity.

Replace Whole-Group Activities with Learning Centers

Learning centers allow more engagement and the opportunity for you to work with small groups or hold individual conferences. They require careful planning and teaching procedures. You have various choices in structuring learning center activities, depending on how much choice and control you give children.

Free-choice centers. The least amount of structure is *Free Choice* in which you allow the children to choose any center they want, any partner, and to stay in that center for as long as they want. It provides children with the chance to learn how to make good choices, and this structure is based on the belief that children know best what they need to learn . You will have a busy, active classroom, with plenty of talking, playing, and interactions. Although free choice centers are more common in preschool, they are appropriate and beneficial for all grades.

Mixed-choice centers. Children are required to complete certain specific center activities and when they're done they can have free choice of other centers. This can be a helpful format when specific activities are required as part of your reading or math series. As a new teacher, you can check the teacher's guides that come with these series for activity ideas. There are often materials and plans for work stations or centers included.

This format also works well when you want the children to participate in a science experiment or art activity that is too difficult to do in a whole group. For example, imagine that you want the children to plant seeds and observe their growth. Rather than having soil, cups, seeds, and tools for all the children to use at once (which can be a real management challenge) you can set this activity up as a learning center. The children can come over to work in pairs or small groups and you will have less mess and more chance to interact with the children, asking questions to stimulate critical thinking.

Teacher-planned centers. The children are assigned to various centers and then after a set period of time, say 15 minutes, they rotate to a different center. The advantage of this is that you can ensure that the children have all been exposed to the same material. The disadvantages, however, are important enough to consider loosening up this structure after the children get used to the procedures and routines. The children don't learn how to make choices or become self-directed. They also do not get the freedom to go deeply into an activity, or decide how much time they want to spend on an activity. This can lead to management problems when children are reluctant to stop working, or when it takes children an extended period of time to get started in their work. They may not get to

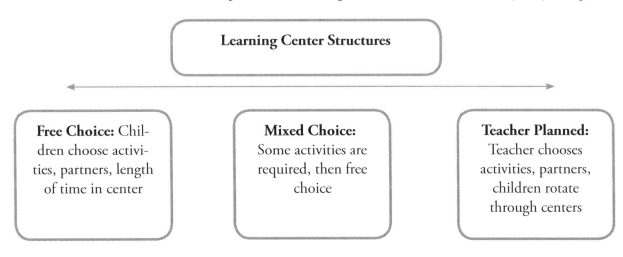

accomplish much. On the other hand, if your school has a rigid curriculum with many lessons that are required each day, this structure is also preferable to a large group setting for reading or math in that it gives you the opportunity to work individually or with small groups of children to differentiate instruction.

Plan Learning Center Activities

The better prepared you are before center time starts, the smoother things will go. Here's a list of the questions you might consider in your planning to help you figure out what behaviors children need to learn and what you need to have ready before class begins.

- *Where does each child go?* Think about how children will know where they will go when center time begins. If you are using free choice, you will still want to have a planning time. This can be done in a small group and plans can be written or oral. The planning helps children to learn how to make choices and to self-regulate their actions. In some classrooms children can wear a colored clothespin that is the same color as the sign of their center. Other classrooms use necklaces or name tags that are placed in the center. Some teachers limit the number of children in each center by having a limited number of hooks available. If you are using assigned centers, primary grade children respond well to charts that show what center they begin with. Click here for a video of managing centers in kindergarten and here for a video of fifth grade centers during guided reading.

- *What do children do when they get there?* Be clear what activities children will do in each center and how they will use the materials or record what they have done. Next, teach the children the procedures for each and every center. Mini-lessons during group time are one way to show children what is available to them and how to use the materials. For example, if you have storytelling props in the library corner, you will want to carry out the story telling and have the children practice using the props during your group reading time.

- *What do children do if they need help?* One of your goals for center time is to help children learn to work independently without your help. This frees you up to work with small groups or individuals. Be sure children know these strategies well before starting learning centers. Here are some popular strategies:

    - Ask three then me. Children are taught to ask three other people—peers or adults—for assistance before going to the teacher

    - *Stop sign.* Have a visual signal that shows STOP or DO NOT DISTURB that you can post when you are working with a small group. When children interrupt, point to the sign and gently redirect them to someone else who can help them, or to try on their own. Make it clear that you will *not* interact with other children while you are working in a "teacher group."

    - *Alternative work.* If a child can't figure out how to do a particular question or activity, have an alternative problem, activity, or worksheet that is available. You can also teach children to just go to the next problem or step in the activity if they get stuck.

- *Emergencies.* Teach children they can only <u>interrupt you for an emergency</u> and teach them what an "emergency" is. For very young children, role play can help them understand this concept; for example, if someone is hurt or sick, fire, smoke, etc.

- *Out of bounds.* Designate a specific area that is the teacher group area. Mark off the area with tape on the floor and teach the children that it is out of bounds during center time.

• *Where do they put their work when they are done?* If you want the children to record their work or save any of the finished products they created during centers, you will need to think through where they will put their work. This could be inside their cubbies, labeled shelves or bins for each child, or for elementary children this could be a specific folder to put work in, a "center-time journal," or binder.

• <u>*What do they do if they finish early?*</u> If you are rotating through centers, children will need to have activities available that they can work on if they finish before it's time to move to the next center, or before center time is over. This might be puzzles and games that they can get from a specific place, or other follow-up activities that children particularly enjoy. This is less of an issue if you are using free choice centers.

• *How do they know when and where to go to the next activity?* If you have free choice centers, children will be able to move from one activity to the next. However, you might still want them to take a moment to clean up what they were working with, check their center time plans, and possibly record what they have done with a drawing or writing. If you are rotating centers, you will want to give children a warning before it is time to switch centers so that children can emotionally prepare themselves as well as finish up what they've been doing. Then you will need a clear signal for when it is time to change. Practice these changes between centers so that children can do them quickly and smoothly. Also make sure children know exactly where they go when they rotate centers. This will increase the children's time on task and keep management problems to a minimum.

Center Time Planning Worksheet

Type of Center Time:

☐ Free Choice   ☐ Mixed Choice
☐ Teacher Planned

List of Centers Available:

1. _____

2. _____

3. _____

4. _____

5. _____

6. _____

7. _____

8. _____

Center Assignments (Where does each child go):

Center Time Planning Worksheet

What do children do if they need help?

_____

_____

_____

_____

Where do children record their work or put their work when done?

_____

_____

_____

_____

What do children do if they finish early?

_____

_____

_____

_____

Learning Center Activity Plan

Name of Center: _____

Objectives: _____

_____

_____

Level of Difficulty: ☐ Beginner   ☐ Intermediate   ☐ Advanced

Materials Needed: _____

_____

_____

Procedures: _____

_____

_____

_____

_____

_____

_____

Assessment: _____

_____

_____

_____

_____

Be Prepared

It is hard to overestimate how important it is to be prepared ahead of time for your lessons and activities. I have seen student teachers repeatedly struggle with children's inattentive behavior or a chaotic lesson because they did not have all their materials ready, or they hadn't thought through the steps they'd use. How will you start the activity? If the children need to move, how will they do this? Where will you put your materials? How will you get them ready while the children are transitioning?

Whether you are doing movement activities with preschoolers at circle time, or reviewing a math lesson in third grade, you will still benefit from writing out the details of what you plan to do. Lesson plans or activity plans are not designed to torture you, but rather to help you learn to think through both the learning goals and the management of the activity. Make a list of the materials you will need and figure out when you will gather them and where you will put them. Also take time to get yourself mentally ready for the activity. Teaching is very complicated because there are so many things to think about simultaneously. Before starting, find a moment to breathe, smile, and go through the steps you will be doing in your head.

Step 4 Checklist for Engaging Children in Learning

- ☐ Choose an appropriate format for activities. Consider alternatives to whole-group instruction
- ☐ Use effective questioning strategies
- ☐ Practice alternatives to hand-raising such as Turn-and-Talk
- ☐ Plan effective seatwork strategies
- ☐ Convert whole-group lessons to learning centers
- ☐ Implement cooperative learning activities
- ☐ Be prepared for all lessons

The Positive Classroom Approach

Step 5: Guide Children's Behavior

In early childhood education, we have a long history of using a guidance approach to behavior management. This means that we view children's behavior through a developmental lens, seeing "misbehavior" as "mistaken behavior" or behavior that serves a purpose for the child in order to get his or her needs met (Gartrell, 2010). This means you need to teach the behavioral skills children need rather than punishing them for what they do inappropriately. Simply put, punishment is not effective for changing children's behavior in the long run, and it can lead to humiliation and emotional pain.

Behavior can be understood as a form of communication. Instead of jumping to the conclusion that the child is wrong, it is helpful first to look at the social, physical, academic and emotional environment in the classroom. Have the children been sitting too long? Is the space too crowded? Are the activities too challenging? Not challenging enough? Is the child hungry, tired, or not feeling well? A great deal of inappropriate behavior occurs because of the classroom context, not because there is something deficient in the child. Sometimes our efforts as teachers cause inappropriate behavior from children. That's why it's so important to teach procedures, build community and teach school success skills first. Don't jump into trying to correct student behavior without a thorough review of your own classroom practices.

Only Respond as Much as Necessary

If at all possible, it is best to intervene as little as possible to allow children to develop their own ability to problem solve. The Teacher Behavior Continuum, shown in the following figure, contains a range of different possible teacher responses to inappropriate behavior (Wolfgang & Glickman, 1986).

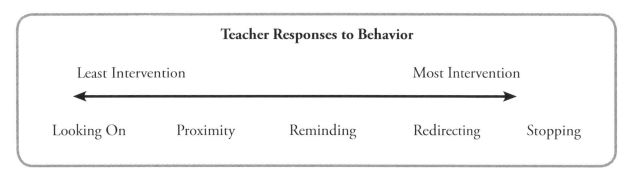

Looking on. Before you intervene, you can observe closely and see whether or not you are needed. By watching carefully, you will also be ready to step in if it becomes necessary. Learn what to let go.

For example, Barbara was watching her 4-year old preschoolers playing in the housekeeping area during work time. She noticed Benjamin and Steven standing next to each other, pretending to prepare a meal. Benjamin wanted a spatula that Steven had and began grabbing it as Steven resisted. Barbara moved closer but said nothing and watched. The two boys struggled for a few moments, each pulling on an end of the spatula. Finally Benjamin relented and said, "Okay, you can have it. I'm gonna make soup." He walked away to get some other materials, then joined Steven again at the counter.

The two boys continued playing and talking as if nothing happened. Barbara made a mental note to work one-on-one later with Benjamin to model how to ask for a turn, rather than grabbing.

Proximity. Just moving closer to a child engaging in inappropriate behavior may help the child to make a different choice or be more mindful of her actions.

For example, if a child is not paying attention, or disturbing another child next to her, you can simply stand closer to her desk or table. Likewise, if children are arguing with each other, you could walk over close to them and just quietly watch. Your presence will encourage children to think differently about their actions.

Redirecting. Redirecting a child's behavior is a way of subtly teaching them a more appropriate behavior that gets the same result. Much misbehavior is the result of children not having the skills or knowledge to get their needs met in a socially safe and acceptable way. That is why we work so hard to get children to "use words" instead of actions when they are unhappy or when they want something.

Imagine four first-graders working at a group math game at their desks that are pushed together. Shanika is moving her piece and Tanya starts getting books out of her desk. The teacher moves over next to Tanya, and gently places her hand on Tanya's books and shakes her head. Tanya puts the books away, and the teacher says, "Tanya, I think it's your turn now." She walks away, but continues to watch the group out of the corner of her eye.

Stopping. There are times when children's behavior is dangerous to themselves or others and they must be stopped immediately. Stopping children's behavior must be done **without anger or humiliation**. Keeping calm yourself is the best guarantee that you will be effective with the child. Once the behavior has stopped, your next step is to use other guidance techniques to ensure that the child will calm down and be able to learn more appropriate behavior.

For example, while you are modeling a science experiment for a first grade class, you notice that Keith has taken out a pencil and is jabbing Latisha in the arm with it. Without too much attention being drawn to the incident, you gently take the pencil away from Keith and ask him to move away from Latisha to a spot farther away from the group. After the group time is over, you can spend some time with Keith problem-solving this behavior and considering other positive behavioral supports.

Teach Children to Resolve Conflicts

Minor conflicts between children are an inevitable part of social relationships. We need to teach children how to manage and resolve minor clashes, arguments, and disagreements. It's important to intervene quickly to teach problem solving skills that will create a more peaceful classroom and teach social skills that children will use throughout their lives.

Epstein (2009) provides the following step-by-step process to teach children problem solving skills:

The Positive Classroom Approach

Problem Solving Steps

1. ***Establish safety.*** Stay calm and stop any actions that could hurt someone. Your ability to stay calm and collected is very important in modeling social skills for the children and for being able to think clearly yourself. For example, first-graders Dylan and Matthew are arguing during center time. Matthew is grabbing a game that is in Dylan's hands. You gently put your arm on Matthew's shoulder and separate the two boys.

2. ***Acknowledge the children's feelings.*** Describing the child's feelings helps the children to be able to listen to you, identify his feelings, and learn how feelings lead to behaviors and consequences. "Matthew, I can tell you are very angry right now. And Dylan, you seem to be scared that Matthew will hurt you." As children get better at this process, you should ask the children to interpret others' feelings: "Matthew, how do you think Dylan is feeling right now?" "Dylan, how do you think Matthew is feeling?"

3. ***Gather information.*** Allow the children to explain their view points, even if you observed the actions. Do not take sides. You will be modeling for the children how to think through problems. "Dylan, can you tell me what happened?" Dylan begins and Matthew interrupts. "Matthew, as soon as he is done, you can tell me what happened, too." Dylan says that Matthew tried to take the game he was using and he had it first. "Okay, Matthew, it's your turn to tell us what happened." Matthew says, "I really want to play with that. I didn't get a turn in forever. And Dylan won't share with me."

4. ***Restate the problem.*** Describe the problem without judgment. Do not use terms like inconsiderate, selfish, stubborn. Just describe what happened. This allows the children to know that they have been heard and understood, and it helps them to see the problem more clearly. "So, it sounds like Dylan was playing with this game and Matthew really wanted a turn with it. Dylan was not ready to share, and Matthew tried to take the game so he could have a turn."

5. ***Ask for solutions.*** Since the goal is to teach social-relationship skills, allow the children to generate possible solutions rather than just pronouncing a solution yourself. If the children come up with the ideas themselves, they are more likely to follow them, and to learn how to eventually do this on their own. "Matthew and Dylan, do you have any suggestions for how we can solve this problem?" Dylan says, "He should leave me alone. I had it first." "Okay, is that a good idea or not?" Matthew chimes in, "No, I want a turn too. How about I get a turn in five minutes?" "That's one idea. Any others?" Dylan suggests, "We could play the game together." Okay, that's another idea. Which idea do you want to try? Matthew says, "Okay, let's play it together. But I get the game first tomorrow." How does that sound, Dylan? "Okay."

6. ***Provide follow-up support.*** After a problem-solving choice is made, check back with the children to be sure the solution is being followed and is working. Give positive feedback to let them know how well they've worked at problem-solving. "Matthew and Dylan, how is your solution working?" "Okay. Jesse wanted to play, too, so we're all gonna play it now." "Great thinking. You did a terrific job of solving this problem." In your feedback, focus on the good job they did with the process, rather than the good idea itself. We want to teach children that the problem-solving process is the important issue.

Post the following list of problem solving steps on the classroom wall to help you remember how to do effective problem solving:

Problem Solving Steps

1. Establish Safety

2. Acknowledge the Children's Feelings

3. Gather Information

4. Restate the Problem

5. Ask for Solutions

6. Provide Follow-up Support

Stop Using Time Out

One of the strategies that was often advocated in years past was the use of "time-out" and especially a "time-out chair." When children used inappropriate behavior, they were sent to a chair or other location that was separate from the group and quiet. Children are often admonished to think about what they did while in time-out, and teachers typically control the amount of time spent isolated. When time-out was advocated as a humane strategy, it was intended to help parents and teachers find an alternative to corporal punishment—hitting, and spanking, for example. While I would certainly agree that time-out is a more humane strategy than corporal punishment, it is not appropriate for helping children develop more positive behaviors.

Isolating children is almost always a painful psychological experience. Children who are often sent to time-out develop a reputation for being a trouble-maker or bad kid. They often internalize these judgments about themselves and become anxious and depressed. As children begin to see themselves as a bad kid or as a trouble-maker, they act in ways that fit that inner view of themselves. The label becomes a self-fulfilling prophecy.

It is also possible that time-out is serving a positive function for the child. If his inappropriate behavior is used in order to get him out of something (like clean-up time, or seatwork in math) then the child might actually prefer time-out. Even if this is not on a conscious level for the child, it is possible that the teacher's actions in sending the child to time-out will increase his or her inappropriate behavior.

Time-out is not successful because it does not teach children what positive behavior or skills they need to learn. When a child misbehaves, focus on teaching her what she should do instead of focusing on what she did wrong. Instead of time-out, use a quiet corner to help children learn to self-regulate and gain control.

Use a Quiet Corner

Children need a <u>positive place to calm down</u> and gain self-control. Create a warm, comforting space in your classroom and give it a name such as, "Quiet Corner." Choose a place in the room such as a comfortable chair, carpet square, pillows, or other spot that is removed from the action, but not really isolated.

Help the children understand the purpose of this time. Explain that we all need help from time to time in learning how to make good choices. We have strong impulses that make us choose what we want to do instead of what we have to do. Going to the Quiet Corner is for a short period to <u>calm down and think</u> about a better choice. Model for the children how the Quiet Corner will work. You might want to give a child a brief reminder of appropriate behavior before sending a child to the Quiet Corner and then if the behavior reoccurs, a Quiet Corner signal should be used. This can be a hand gesture, such as pointing to the area, sign language, or a simple phrase such as, "Please go to the Quiet Corner Jaqueline." The child should be taught to go immediately, without protest or explanation. Once the child has regained control she can let you know if she needs to explain her behavior, but not when she is told to go. Children can also choose to use the Quiet Corner when they need to calm themselves down, or to get away for a minute or two. Obviously, you should not let children "escape" in the Quiet Corner and avoid academic activities, but it can be very helpful in getting a child to relax and get back to work.

The child should ideally decide when to return to the group's activities, however with younger children you will need to monitor this to make the time concrete. A minute or two is usually plenty. Also teach the class how to help someone who is taking a break by leaving him alone and continuing one's work. Once you've modeled this process, have the children practice it. You can go to the Quiet Corner as well, to get across the idea that we all need support at times.

Model what a child should be doing when taking a break. Teach children how to take deep breaths to calm their bodies and minds. Pretend to be in the Quiet Corner and model your thinking out loud, especially calming down, gaining control, and making a good choice.

The most critical aspect of using the Quiet Corner as a positive process is your attitude and tone of voice. Children can tell when you are annoyed and frustrated and then this will turn into an ineffective punishment. You don't want this to be Time-Out. Have the child use the Quiet Corner when you first see any agitation so he can calm down before the inappropriate behavior gets out of hand. For example, you might have a child use the Quiet Corner when he is talking during quiet seat work, poking another child at circle time, pushing others during transitions, or using materials inappropriately.

Be sure to welcome the child back to the class activities in a positive way. Show the child that he is cared for and an important part of the group and get the child involved in work right away. Some children might need a discussion with you later about why they needed a break and how they might behavior more appropriately in the future. The focus should always be on what better choice the child can make. Instead of "think about what you did" the child should be encouraged to "calm down and think about what you need to do now."

Set and Enforce Limits

It is your job as a teacher to let children know when their behavior is not appropriate. This is sometimes difficult for new teachers because they are afraid of "being mean" to the children and not being liked. Rest assured, though, that you do not need to scream, punish or be mean in order to set limits. In fact, children will appreciate knowing that someone will help them learn control because it is a frightening world when any behavior is allowed. Limits on behavior help children develop a personal understanding of what is right and wrong.

You can apply consequences to children's actions to help them understand the effects of their behaviors. Choose a sanction that is directly related to the misbehavior. These sanctions can include exclusion, deprivation, and restitution (DeVries & Zan, 1994). Always be careful that children are not humiliated. The focus should be on what the child can learn, rather than punishment. Two strategies are critical for this to be successful:

1. Stay calm. Be sure that you are emotionally calm and can deliver the message in a matter-of-fact tone. One effective strategy is the STAR Technique (Bailey, 2001):

> **STAR Technique:**
>
> **S**mile
> **T**ake a Breath
> **A**nd
> **R**elax

2. Give a second chance. Offer the child another chance later to demonstrate positive behaviors.

Use Natural Consequences

Not all conflict needs your intervention. Natural consequences occur without teacher intervention. In fact, the most challenging part of using natural consequences is knowing when to allow children to experience the consequences. Of course, if children are in imminent danger of hurting themselves, other people, or school materials, you must stop the behavior immediately. Many times, however, children can and will figure things out themselves. Be sure that the children are actually learning something from the consequences of their behavior, rather than just suffering frustration or humiliation. It is never appropriate for natural consequences to be harsh or unsafe.

Examples of Natural Consequences

- *Stop that!* Ms. Price watched as Naomi, playing at the water table, tried to sprinkle water on Devon's arms. Devon shouted, "Stop that. You're getting me all wet!" Naomi stopped, and went back to pouring water into the buckets. She then said to Devon, "I've got lemonade. You want some?" In this interaction, Devon, a boy with especially good

social skills, effectively set limits for Naomi. Naomi got the message and quickly tried a different approach at engaging Devon in her play.

- *You can't play!* Keon is working with a group of 2nd grade boys in the math center and he refuses to let the others use the materials. Jason cries, "You're not gonna play with us when we go outside!" Keon frowns and his face shows anger and frustration, as he turns away, hoarding the materials. You wait to see what happens. The other boys continue talking, and a few minutes later, Keon pushes the materials into the middle of the table so they can all use them. When you look over a while later, the group is working well without conflict. While certainly Jason's remark was painful, Keon was able to connect the cause and effect relationship of his hording the materials to Jason's outburst.

Use Exclusion when Appropriate

When children are not able to adhere to the behaviors needed to participate in social activities, you can exclude them as a way of teaching them the boundaries for the behavior.

Examples of Exclusion:

- *Leave the sandbox:* Keyana is sitting in the sandbox and she excitedly throws the sand up in the air over and over again. You rush over. "Keyana, you must stop throwing the sand in the air, it can hurt children's eyes. We don't hurt others." A few minutes later you see Keyana return to her previous actions, throwing the sand higher. You say to her in a calm tone, "Keyana, I see you are having a hard time playing safely with the sand. You will need to leave the sandbox so our friends are all safe. Tomorrow you can try again to see if you can play safely." You help Keyana choose a different activity, gently guiding her out of the sandbox.

- *Go to the Quiet Corner.* Brian came back after lunch very irritable and had been arguing with his classmates during center time. His teacher reminded him twice about working cooperatively and modeled positive things to say. A few minutes later, Brian pushed Michael and knocked off some of the materials on the table. The teacher calmly approached and said, "Brian, it looks like you are frustrated and angry (acknowledging feelings). I can't let you disturb the other children who are working or damage our materials. Please go to the Quiet Corner until you feel ready to join the group again." Notice that his teacher did not impose a time limit on how long he needed to stay there. This was a powerful way of giving control back to Brian and allowing him to practice self-regulating.

Use Deprivation When Appropriate

An effective way to teach children how to treat materials is to take away the opportunity to use them for a short while. First, make sure that children know what behaviors are expected. They might need individualized, direct instruction and modeling to learn these expectations. Next, they need to know that you are serious about the expectations and that you will enforce them. As always, this needs to be done without any anger or frustration in your voice. Think of this as teaching the limits of behavior rather than punishment.

Examples of Deprivation

- ***Using markers correctly.*** A first-grade teacher was having a difficult time getting Hannah to remember to put the covers on the markers. After repeated attempts to show her how to make sure the caps are on and click shut, Hannah was still tossing the markers into the bin on her table without the covers on. Her teacher approached her and said in a calm voice, "Hannah, I see you are having trouble using the markers properly. I can't let them be ruined since everyone enjoys them. Today you will need to use your pencil or crayons instead. We'll try the markers again this afternoon to see if you are able to take care of them." The teacher moved the markers away, and put down a pack of crayons next to her.

- ***Flying rubberbands.*** Jake was enthusiastic about using the geoboards to make patterns during math. Even when shown the proper way to use the rubber bands, he continued to shoot them around the room. His teacher, Ms. Winston, gently took away the board and rubber bands. "Jake, you haven't yet learned how to use the geoboards properly so today you can use paper and pencil to make your patterns. Tomorrow we will try again to see if you can use the rubber bands safely so that no-one gets hurt."

Use Restitution When Appropriate

Teach children how to make amends when they have made the wrong choices in their behaviors. This is the essence of relationship-building and an important aspect of being a mature person. Rather than punishing a child for an action, it is a better learning experience for her to see that she has caused a problem and should then fix it. This strategy can be applied to a wide variety of situations, such as when one child hurts another child. Restitution can also be used in conjunction with the other strategies described above.

Examples of Restitution

- ***Make someone feel better.*** Annie has just knocked over Frankie's block structure as she dashed through the block area in her preschool. Her teacher gently stops her and points out that she has damaged Frankie's work. "See, Frankie is very sad that all his work has been knocked down because you rushed through this area. What can you do to make Frankie feel better?" Perhaps Annie will offer to help Frankie rebuild the structure, or give him a hug. The teacher asked Frankie what would work best for him and then guided Annie in following up on her restitution.

- ***Fix what is broken.*** After Asad ripped one of the classroom books in anger, the teacher calmly dealt with his behavior (by teaching breathing strategies for him to calm down before he gets so angry) and had Asad tape the pages of the book to fix them.

When you use any kind of consequences, be sure you use a calm, matter-of-fact voice and be sure that the child understands the cause and effect relationship. Never use sarcasm, humiliation, or harm. Your message must be that the behavior is unacceptable, but the child is cared about. Continue to work on building and maintaining a strong relationship with the child, even when using consequences. If you find that you have strong emotions building up, use a calming technique for yourself before intervening.

> **Teacher Applied Consequences:**
> - **Exclusion (Can't participate)**
> - **Deprivation (Can't use materials)**
> - **Restitution (Makes amends)**

Help Attention-Seeking Children

"Ignore him—he just wants attention!" Attention-seeking behavior has a bad reputation in our schools, and it can often lead to difficult classroom management challenges. Seeking attention is a way of getting our love and belongingness needs met. The need for human interaction and affection is so strong that it is a kind of hunger—the more a child lacks these interactions, the harder he will try to get them. Any interactions, even negative ones, are better than none. Many children act out in order to get the social interaction with the teacher that they need. Often a child with frequent misbehavior is sent to a vice principal, center director, or other disciplinarian, where he gets additional one-on-one attention. In any case, the typical result of attention-seeking behavior is, not surprisingly, lots of attention!

So wouldn't it make sense to ignore these behaviors to stop reinforcing them? Yes, but only if you ***increase*** the amount of positive attention the child gets at other times. The child is hungry for a relationship with you and it can be difficult to develop this if you are angry and frustrated with the child. What to do instead? Check out the worksheet below:

Worksheet for Helping Attention-Seeking Children

1. Schedule time. Plan when you will be able to spend time with the child. Sit next to him at snack or invite him to read to you one-on-one. Greet him warmly when he arrives and spend an extra minute talking with him at the end of the day. Have honest, authentic interactions. Find out more about his likes, habits, fears, and hopes. Think about connecting.

Interactions planned: _____

_____

Time of interactions: _____

2. Plan social interactions. Plan ways he can interact with other children in a successful way. Pair him up with a child who has excellent social skills for buddy activities.

Possible Buddies: _____

_____

Buddy Activities: _____

_____

3. Send home positive notes. Once a week, send a note that describes a couple of positive things that the child did that week. Do not share the minor negative issues.

Day to send note home weekly: _____

4. Help connect child to other adults. Ask the child to bring a note to the office, help the teacher assistant set up lunch, or spend time with the librarian putting books away.

Plan for Connecting to Other Adults: _____

_____

Understand and Intervene in the Acting-Out Cycle

In order to understand children's challenging behaviors, it's helpful to take a closer look at what is going on when children act out in behaviors such as screaming, throwing things, fighting, or tantrums. It may seem like this behavior comes out of nowhere, but in reality, there are phases in this acting out cycle that are recognizable and predictable (The IRIS Center for Training Enhancements, n.d.-a). When you learn to identify the phases in this cycle, you can intervene earlier and help children learn new behaviors and skills, and adapt your teaching and classroom to be more supportive.

The figure below shows the seven steps of the acting out cycle, demonstrating how the intensity builds and accelerates into a peak and then subsides. Your goal is to help the child in the early stages of the cycle, preventing the full cycle from occurring. Your response to the child's acting out cycle will completely depend on what point in the cycle you are intervening.

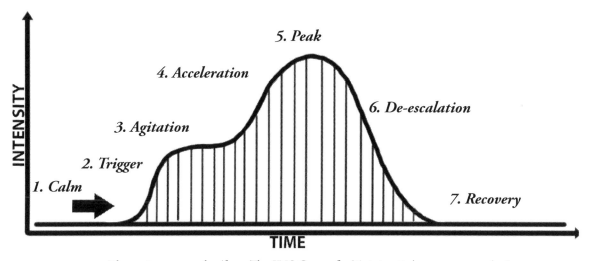

The acting out cycle. (from The IRIS Center for Training Enhancements, n.d.-a)

Calm phase. Children who are in the calm phase are typically engaged in learning, able to socialize comfortably, focus attention, and respond to requests. Most of the strategies in this book are designed to help keep children in the calm phase, however teaching social and emotional skills are especially important. It is also critical to create a positive climate by building relationships and giving children plenty of attention. It's helpful to remember that some children may typically be in an anxious state on a regular basis and will need more support to achieve calmness.

Trigger. Children's behavior can change as a result of classroom triggers such as a change in the routine, a negative interaction with the children or teacher, confusion about an activity, or overwhelming stimulation. Besides the classroom environment, children may be triggered because of hunger, not getting enough sleep, oncoming illness, or stress at home. As you get to know your children, pay special attention to what their specific triggers might be.

The first strategy you can use is to help the child avoid or manage his triggers. For example, if you know that Kevin tends to get angry and hit children when the class is coming in from recess, you can use some prevention strategies such as asking Kevin to come in for a special job ahead of the rest of the class. Or you can walk next to Kevin, engaging him in conversation as you enter the classroom. If you know that Jenny begins to have tantrums at the beginning of clean-up time, you can give her early notice that center time is ending, or get her to stop ahead of the other children and then give her a job to do—like watering the plants—that is away from all the movement during clean up time. When triggers are related to health issues or the home environment, you'll want to share information with families to help reduce triggers. For example, parents might not realize their child is tired or hungry during the day.

Agitation phase. After a trigger occurs, a child will begin to get agitated. In my view this is the critical phase that requires your intervention. At this point, children's emotions and behaviors begin to gain energy. If you are attuned to this phase, you may notice nail biting, hair twirling, tapping, wiggling, inability to sit still, a lack of focus, or daydreaming. Some children will clench their fists, or their jaw, making a grimace or showing frustration on their face. It is critical to be able to recognize and intervene at the trigger or the agitation phase to prevent behaviors that end up being aggressive. At this point intervention by the teacher is the most effective and most necessary.

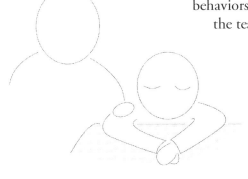

Your goal in the agitation phase is to restore calm, otherwise the child will move into the acceleration phase and can become out of control. It's especially important not to yell at the child or add to their growing tension with lecturing or reprimands. Calming a child in the agitation phase can be as simple as moving your body close by, giving some focused attention on the child, or redirecting the child toward a different activity. Here are some examples:

- ☐ 4-year old Carmen is playing in the housekeeping area and two other girls move close to her to play with the kitchen items. Carmen makes an angry face and starts to push their things off the table. You quickly walk over and engage Carmen in a conversation about her play. She starts to relax and smile so you make suggestions about playing together with the other girls.

- ☐ You have just finished guided reading in a 2nd grade classroom and the children are going back to their desks to start journal writing. Michael, who is typically overwhelmed by writing, begins with a few words but gets frustrated, tears out the page and crumples it up. You walk over quickly and calmly and talk to him about his writing ideas. He chooses an idea and you suggest he just writes a couple of words and then you'll come back over and check in with him. Michael begins writing again and is able to complete a full sentence.

- ☐ Tyler, a kindergartner, has been engaged and sitting quietly throughout the shared reading time. Toward the end of the book, he begins to fidget on the carpet and starts rocking his body side to side. You notice this and call on Tyler to come up and point to one of the words in the Big Book that starts with the same letter as his name. He quickly gets up and bounces to the front of the carpet.

The most important thing to keep in mind is reducing the negative energy and restoring calm. If at this phase, for example, you reprimanded Michael for tearing up the paper, or yelled at Tyler to sit still, it could easily have pushed the child into the acceleration phase rather than restoring calm. You can talk to the child later about the problem behavior, or help her learn new coping strategies, but at this point, your only goal is to restore calm.

Acceleration phase. The child increases his efforts to engage the teacher, often through arguing, refusing to do what was asked, and perhaps beginning to push or kick other children or throw things. During this phase children start to use negative behaviors to gain the teacher's attention. It is a form of communication which says "Help me!" For novice teachers, this is often the first part of the cycle noticed as being problematic, which is why it is so important to practice recognizing triggers and agitation. It is much easier to redirect a child and keep a positive focus before the acceleration phase because young children's behavior and composure can fall apart quickly.

Once again, you need to cool things off and calm the child down, even if it means ignoring some of these behaviors for the time being. The worst thing a teacher can do at this point is engage in a power struggle. This adds tension and intensity to the child's emotional state and will push the child right into the peak phase. Imagine the child's behavior as a run-away train. We can either help put on the brakes, or add fuel to the engine that pushes it into worse behavior. Here are some examples:

- ☐ First grader, Kaylie, is working with two other children at their desks, putting together a word puzzle. She begins to get frustrated when she is not able to take over control of the puzzle, whining at the girls, and jumping out of her seat. The teacher is helping children across the room and doesn't notice this until Kaylie yells at the girls, "I wanna do it myself!" and sweeps some of the pieces off onto the floor. The teacher notices this and asks her to pick them up. Kaylie responds, stamping her feet, "No, I won't. You can't make me." The teacher calmly approaches her and, with a neutral tone of voice, she asks Kaylie to come for a walk with her. She takes her to the hallway and suggests she gets a drink of water. As Kaylie calms down, the teacher is able to talk with her about problem-solving strategies that might work with the other girls.

- ☐ Three-year old Jackson is playing with the blocks, trying to build a large tower. Mark comes over and places a block on top of his tower. Jackson screams, "Stop it! My tower," and the boy moves away. The teacher is in the art area, and doesn't notice Jackson's agitation. A few minutes later, Mark returns to the area, and tries again to place a block on Jackson's tower. Jackson screams, "Stop it!" and pushes Mark away, causing him to tumble backwards. The teacher quickly comes over and with a calm, soothing voice says, "Jackson, you've got a lot of blocks on that tower." She sits down next to him, between him and Mark and puts her hand on his shoulder. "It looks like you really want to work on this tower by yourself." As Jackson shows signs of calming down, she prompts, "Jackson, can you say to Mark, 'I want to work alone?'" He repeats this and she turns to Mark to help him find another activity.

- ☐ Jorge, a second grader, begins to wriggle on the rug while the teacher reads a story and asks the class questions. He begins to call out answers and his teacher reminds him to raise his hand. He continues to wriggle around on the rug, bumping into the children next to him. He calls out a few more times, but does not get the teacher's attention. He starts to poke the boy next to him who yells out, "Stop it! That hurt!" The teacher calmly asks Jorge to come sit next to her, and she decides to get out individual white boards for the children to write answers on instead of calling on children to respond. Jorge takes the board with a smile on his face. Later she will work with him on ways he can let her know when he needs a break from sitting on the rug at reading time.

What do all these examples have in common? The teacher stayed calm in both tone of voice and body language. She redirected the child each time, rather than tackling head-on the behavior problem. If the teacher had started to argue with Kaylie about picking up the puzzle pieces, or spoke in a harsh voice to Jackson about pushing Mark, or punished Jorge by making him leave the rug, these children would have likely ramped up their own behavior into full-blown outbursts.

The hardest part of this strategy is letting go of the idea that all inappropriate behavior must be corrected, punished, or dealt with immediately. When children are this agitated, the most important step is to cool them down so they can think and act more appropriately. The time to teach a child more appropriate behaviors is not when he is upset. When the child's anger is directed at us, rather than another child, this can be especially hard to do. With practice, being able to stay calm and redirect children's behavior during the Acceleration Phase will pay off in fewer severely inappropriate behaviors. You will also be more effective in teaching children appropriate behaviors to use instead.

Peak phase. At this point in the cycle the child is out of control. You will now be unable to prevent the problem behavior and must try to reduce the harm as much as possible. Think of a plan ahead of time for out-of-control behavior so that all the adults in the room know how to respond. Check with your school or center to find out if there are preferred procedures for what to do when a child is out of control. This is often the point at which we get very stressed—even frightened of children's behavior. Practice ahead of time using breathing techniques, positive thoughts ("I can handle this"), or other self-calming behaviors. It is essential to stay as calm as you can because your anxiety and negative energy will transfer to the child. The child needs *you* to stay calm in order to regain control! Lecturing, admonishing, yelling at, or threatening the child at this point will only prolong the behavior. Try calming techniques with the child, and if necessary, move the child to a safe place away from the rest of the children. The peak phase is usually intense but short-lived—if you don't add negative energy to it.

First, act to ensure that everyone is safe from harm. You may need to gently but firmly restrain a child from hurting himself or others. Your focus is to help the child regain control in a respectful, caring way. It's sometimes hard to remember that a child is literally out of control and that he might not have the skills to calm himself down. At this point the child needs your help and care. The best possible scenario is to move out of this phase quickly and restore order.

De-escalation. After an outburst, children are often disoriented, confused and perhaps exhausted. They usually respond well to your requests at this point and they need a few minutes to regroup. This is a good time to direct the child to the Quiet Corner and encourage her to put on headphones and listen to calming music, hold a comfort item, look at a book, or to just lay her head down. At this point, you will want to return your attention for a couple minutes to the rest of the class to establish order and ensure the other children are engaged again.

Recovery phase. When you return to the child, sit for a minute or two and discuss the situation, trying to learn as much as you can from the child about what triggered his behavior. This is often difficult with preschoolers or younger children, but it can be helpful to hear the child's side of the story. Don't assume that you know what was going in the child's mind. You might start by just saying, "You were very upset just then. What was going on for you?" Don't ask "why" questions since they are often interpreted as accusations. When children begin to realize that you are not interested in finding blame and sentencing them to a punishment, they will be more likely to open up to you. Then you can use this information to better help you identify triggers and agitation. During the recovery phase, you should also help the children make a plan for what to do in the future when the trigger occurs. Be sure to follow up on the plan by teaching how to calm down and by practicing while he is calm.

The Acting Out Cycle
(The IRIS Center for Training Enhancements, n.d.-a)

Phase	Student Behavior	Teacher Response
1. Calm	Children are engaged fully in learning activity; emotional stability and full cognitive focus.	Provide positive attention, work on developing relationships with children, provide safe, calm environment.
2. Trigger	Environmental stressors such as change in schedule, boredom, confusion, over stimulation, negative social interactions; internal stressors such as hunger, lack of sleep, illness, medication, stress at home.	Begin to recognize what triggers are and help to prevent them, change the setting, social interactions, offer positive attention.
3. Agitation Phase	Disengages from activity or lesson; shows body movements of agitation—tapping, rocking, running around—or stares into space, walks around unengaged, stops participating.	Redirect child, change the way the child is working on the activity—offer choices; provide assistance, offer calming techniques.
4. Acceleration Phase	Attempts to gain teacher attention in negative ways: argues, is non-compliant, tests limits, tries to provoke the teacher and/or other children.	Redirect child to appropriate behavior calmly, acknowledge feelings, make high-probability requests; give positive attention. Do not engage in argument, use sarcasm, or offer negative remarks.
5. Peak Phase	Child is out of control; verbal and physical aggression toward teacher and other children; crying, damaging materials.	Maintain safety, stay calm yourself, help child to regain control in respectful caring way.
6. De-escalation Phase	Child is disoriented, confused, tired, and often withdrawn; typically receptive to teacher requests; may blame others and try to reconcile.	Move child to Quiet Corner, provide calm independent activity; check on rest of class to restore order.
7. Recovery Phase	Child is subdued and has calmed down. May avoid talking about the incident.	Debriefing of incident is critical. Discuss what triggered incident and make plan for prevention in future.

Step 5 Checklist for Guiding Behavior

☐ Only respond as much as necessary

☐ Teach children to resolve conflicts

☐ Stop using time out

☐ Use a quiet corner

☐ Set and enforce limits

☐ Use exclusion when appropriate

☐ Use deprivation when appropriate

☐ Use restitution when appropriate

☐ Help attention-seeking children

☐ Understand and intervene in the acting-out cycle

Find Joy in Teaching

Hopefully the suggestions in this book will help you maintain your enthusiasm for teaching, find support when you need it, and prepare for the challenges, stress, and satisfaction of teaching. Teaching should be joyful and meaningful, and if it is not, that doesn't mean you have to accept being miserable. Think through the changes you can make, and give them time to work. If you are still unhappy, it might be time to change where you work, what age group you work with, or even consider a different way to work with children than in the classroom.

As you move on in your career, never lose sight of the fact that you are an important person in the lives of the children you teach and their families. You make an important contribution to your community, and you help create a better world. May you always find joy in these accomplishments!

☙ ☙ ☙

References and Resources

Abdullah, M. H. (2002). Bibliotherapy. *ERIC Clearinghouse on Reading, English and Communication, Digest 177.*

Ackermann, K. Revell, V., Lao, O., Rombouts, E., Skene, D., Kayser, M. (2012). Diurnal rhythms in blood cell populations and the effect of acute sleep deprivation in healthy young men. *Sleep, 35*(7), 933-40.

Ainslie, K. (n.d.). Tips for teachers: Zoning in the preschool classroom. Retrieved May 24, 2010, from http://depts.washington.edu/hscenter/sites/default/files/01_15m_inclusion_inservice/06_zoning/documents/zoning_tips_for_teachers.pdf

Ainsworth-Darnell, J. W., & Downey, D. B. (1998). Assessing the oppositional culture explanation for racial/ethnic differences in school performance. *American Sociological Review, 63,* 536-553.

Alber, S. R., & Heward, W. L. (1997). Recruit it or lose it! Training students to recruit positive teacher attention. *Intervention in School and Clinic, 32,* 275-282.

Alexander, K. L., Entwisle, D. R., & Herman, R. (1999). In the eye of the beholder: Parents' and teachers' ratings of children's behavioral style. In C. L. Shehan (Ed.), *Contemporary perspectives on family research: Vol. 1. Revisioning children as active agents of family life.* Greenwich, CT: JAI Press.

Alexander, K. L., Entwisle, Doris R., & Thompson, Maxine S. (1987). School performance, status relations, and the structure of sentiment: Bringing the teacher back in. *American Sociological Review, 52,* 665-682.

Ashford, J., LeCroy, C. W., & Lortie, K. L. (2006). *Human behavior in the social environment* (3rd ed.). Belmont, CA: Thompson.

Bailey, B. (2001). *Conscious discipline: 7 basic skills for brain smart classroom management.* Oviedo, FL: Loving Guidance, Inc.

Battistich, V., & Watson, M. (2003). Fostering social development in preschool and the early elementary grades through co-operative classroom activities. In R. M. Gillies & A. F. Ashman (Eds.), *Cooperative learning: The social and intellectual outcomes of learning in groups* (pp. 19-35). New York: Routledge.

Beauboeuf-Lafontant, T. (2002). A womanist experience of caring: Understanding the pedagogy of exemplary Black women teachers. *The Urban Review, 34*(1), 71-86.

Beaulieu, C. (2004). Intercultural study of personal space: A case study. *Journal of Applied Social Psychology, 34*(4), 794-805.

Belfiore, P. J., Basile, Pulley, S. & Lee, D. L. (2008). Using a high probability command sequence to increase classroom compliance: The role of behavioral momentum. *Journal of Behavioral Education, 17*(2), 160-171.

Bennett, K. P., & LeCompte, M. D. (1990). *The Way Schools Work: A Sociological Analysis of Education.* New York: Longman.

Bennet, M. & Blundell, D. (1983). Quantity and quality of work in rows and classroom groups. *Educational Psychology, 3*(2), 93-105.

Bermúdez, A. B., & Márquez, J. A. (1996). An examination of a four-way collaborative to increase parental involvement in the school. *The Journal of Educational Issues of Language Minority Students, 16,* 1-10.

Berry, J. W. (1996). *Let's talk about feeling sad.* New York: Scholastic.

Bloom, B. S., & Krathwohl, D. R. (1956). *Taxonomy of educational objectives: The classification of educational goals, by a committee of college and university examiners. Handbook 1: Cognitive domain.* New York: Longman.

Bodrova, E., & Leong, D. J. (2007). *Tools of the mind: The Vygotskian approach to early childhood education* (2nd ed.). Upper Saddle River, NJ: Pearson.

Bodrova, E., & Leong, D. J. (2008). Developing self-regulation in kindergarten: Can we keep the crickets in the basket? *Young Children, 63*(2), 56-58.

Bond, N. (2007). Questioning strategies that minimize classroom management problems. *Kappa Delta Pi, 44*(1), 18-21.

Bondy, E., & Ross, D. D. (2008). The teacher as warm demander. *Educational Leadership, 66*(1), 54-58.

Boykin, A. W. (1978). Psychological/behavioral verve in academic/task performance: Pre-theoretical considerations. *Journal of Negro Education, 47*, 343-354.

Bronson, P., & Merriman, A. (2009). *Nurture shock: New thinking about children.* New York: Hatchett Book Group.

Brophy, J. (2006). History of research on classroom management. In C. M. Evertson & C. S. Weinstein (Eds.), *Handbook of classroom management: Research, practice and contemporary issues* (pp. 17-43). New York: Routledge.

Brown, M., & Ralph, S. (1998). The identification of stress in teachers. In J. D. V. Varma (Ed.), *Stress in teachers: Past, present and future* (pp. 37-56). London: Whurr Publishers Ltd.

Buck, G. H. (1999). Smoothing the rough edges of classroom transitions. *Intervention in School and Clinic, 34*(4), 224-235.

California Services for Technical Assistance and Training (CalSTAT). (2012). Classroom management. Module 4: Teaching students how to behave: Social skills.

Carter, K., & Doyle, W. (2006). Classroom management in early childhood and elementary classrooms. In C. M. Evertson & C. S. Weinstein (Eds.), *Handbook of classroom management: Research, practice and contemporary issues.* New York: Lawrence Erlbaum Associates.

Cazden, C. B. (2001). *Classroom discourse: The language of teaching and learning* (2nd ed.). Portsmouth, NH: Heinemann.

Center on the Social and Emotional Foundations of Learning. (n.d.). *Tucker Turtle Takes Time to Tuck and Think* Retrieved January 6, 2009, from http://www.vanderbilt.edu/csefel/scriptedstories/tuckerturtle.ppt

Chapman, A. (1995-2012). Gender bias in education. *Critical Multicultural Pavillion Research Room.* Retrieved August 20, 2012, from http://www.edchange.org/multicultural/papers/genderbias.html

Chen, X., Rubin, K. H., Cen, G., Hastings, P.D., Chen, H., & Stewart, S.L. (1998). Child-rearing attitudes and behavioral inhibition in Chinese and Canadian toddlers: A cross-cultural study. *Developmental Psychology, 34*(4), 677-686.

Child Welfare Information Gateway. (2007). Recognizing child abuse and neglect: Signs and symptoms. Retrieved July 6, 2010, from http://www.childwelfare.gov/pubs/factsheets/signs.cfm

Child Welfare Information Gateway. (2008). Mandatory reporters of child abuse and neglect. Retrieved July 6, 2010, from http://www.childwelfare.gov/systemwide/laws_policies/statutes/manda.cfm

Chinese for Affirmative Action. (2006). Lost without translation: Language barriers faced by limited-English proficient parents with children in the San Francisco Unified School District. Retrieved January 12, 2011, from http://www.caasf.org/PDFs/Lost%20Without%20Translation%20[CAA].pdf

Cochran-Smith, M. (1991). Learning to teach against the grain. *Harvard Educational Review, 61*(3), 279-310.

Connolly, T., Dowd, T., Criste, A., Nelson, C., & Tobias, L. (1995). *The well-managed classroom: Promoting student success through social skill instruction.* Boys Town, NE: Boys Town Press.

Conroy, M. A. (2005). A descriptive analysis of positive behavioral intervention research with young children with challenging behavior. *Topics in Early Childhood Special Education, 25*(3), 157-166.

Cooper, H. (2007). *The battle over homework: Common ground for administrators, teachers, and parents* (3rd ed.). Thousand Oaks, CA: Corwin.

Cooper, H., Robinson, J. C. & Patall, E. A. (2006). Does homework improve academic achievement? A synthesis of research, 1987–2003. *Review of Educational Research, 76*(1), 1-62.

Cross, T., Bazron, B., Dennis, K., & Isaacs, M. (1989). *Towards a culturally competent system of care, volume I.* Washington, D.C.: Georgetown University Child Development Center, CASSP Technical Assistance Center.

Curtis, J. L.. (1998). *Today I feel silly: And other moods that make my day.* New York HarperCollins.

Daly, P. M., & Ranalli, P. (2003). Using Countoons to teach self-monitoring skills. *Teaching Exceptional Children, 35*(5), 30-35.

Darling-Hammond, L. (2001). The challenge of staffing our schools. *Educational Leadership, 58,* 12-17.

Denham, S.A., Blair, K.A., DeMulder, E., Levitas, J., Sawyer, K., Auerbach-Major, S., & Queenan, P. (2003). Preschool emotional competence: Pathway to social competence. *Child Development, 74*(1), 238-256.

Derman-Sparks, L., & Edwards, J. O. (2010). *Anti-bias education for young children and ourselves.* Washington, DC: National Association for the Education of Young Children.

Devereux Early Childhood Initiative. (2004). *Building protective factors through gross motor game play.* Villanova, PA: Devereux Foundation.

DeVries, R., & Kohlberg, L. (1990). *Constructivist early education: overview and comparison with other programs.* Washington, D.C.: National Association for the Education of Young Children.

DeVries, R., & Zan, B. (1994). *Moral classrooms, moral children: Creating a constructivist atmosphere in early education.* New York: Teachers College Press.

Division of Early Childhood, & National Association for the Education of Young Children. (2009). *Early Childhood Inclusion.* Retrieved May 17, 2010, from http://www.dec-sped.org/uploads/docs/about_dec/position_concept_papers/PositionStatement_Inclusion_Joint_updated_May2009.pdf

Downey, D. B., & Pribesh, S. (2004). When race matters: Teacher's evaluations of students' classroom behavior. *Sociology of Education, 77*(4), 267-282.

Duckworth, A. L., & Seligman, M. E. P. (2005). Self-discipline outdoes IQ in predicting academic performance of adolescents. *Psychological Science, 16*(12), 939-944.

Dunlap, G., Strain, P. S., Fox, L., Carta, J. J., Conroy, M., Smith, B. J., . . . Sowell, C. (2006). Prevention and intervention with young children's challenging behavior: Perspectives regarding current knowledge. *Behavioral Disorders, 32*(1), 29-45.

Dweck, C. S. (2007). The perils and promise of praise. *Educational Leadership, 65*(2), 34-39.

Early Childhood Equity Initiative. (n.d.). *Equity/anti-bias classroom assessment.* Washington, D.C.: Teaching for Change.

Eigsti, I., Zayas, V., Mischel, W., Shoda, Y., Ayduk, O., Dadlani, M. B., Davidson, M. C., . . . Casey, B. J. (2006). Predictive cognitive control from preschool to late adolescence and young adulthood. *Psychological Science, 17*, 478-484.

Emberley, E., & Miranda, A. (1997). *Glad Monster Sad Monster.* Boston: Little Brown and Company.

Emmer, E. T., Evertson, C. M., & Anderson, I. (1980). Effective classroom management at the beginning of the school year. *Elementary School Journal, 80*(5), 219-231.

Epstein, A. (2009). *Me, you, us: Social-emotional learning in preschool.* Ypsilanti, MI: High Scope Press.

Epstein, J. L., & Sanders, M. G. (2002). Family, school, and community partnerships. In M. H. Bornstein (Ed.), *Handbook of parenting, Volume 5: Practice issues in parenting.* Mahwah, NJ: Lawrence Erlbaum.

Evertson, C. M., Anderson, C., Anderson, L., & Brophy, J. (1980). Relationships between classroom behaviors and student outcomes in junior high mathematics and English classes. *American Educational Research Journal, 17*, 43-60.

Evertson, C. M., & Anderson, I. (1979). Beginning school. *Educational Horizons, 57*(4), 164-168.

Evertson, C. M., Emmer, E. T., Clements, B. S., & Worsham, M E. (2008). *Classroom management for elementary teachers* (8th ed.). Boston: Allyn & Bacon.

Faber, A., & Mazlish, E. (1995). *How to talk so kids can learn at home and at school.* NY: Scribner.

Ferguson, C., Ramos, M., Rudo, Z., & Wood, L. (2008). *The school-family connection: Looking at the larger picture: A review of current literature.* Austin, TX: National Center for Family and Community Connections with Schools.

Finders, M., & Lewis, C. (1994). Why some parents don't come to school. *Educational Leadership, 51*(8), 50-54.

Fisher, C, Berliner, D., Filby, N, Marliave, R, Cahen, L, & Dishaw, M. (1978). Teaching behaviors, academic learning time, and student achievement: An overview. In C. Denham & A. Lieberman (Eds.), *Time to learn* (pp. 7-32). Washington, D.C.: U.S. Government Printing Office.

Friedman, I. (2006). Classroom management and teacher stress and burn out. In C. M. Evertson & C. S. Weinstein (Eds.), *Handbook of classroom management: research, practice, and contemporary issues* (pp. 925-944). Mahwah, NJ: Lawrence Erlbaum.

Gartrell, D. (2006). The beauty of class meetings. *Young Children, 61*(6), 54-55.

Gartrell, D. (2010). *A guidance approach for the encouraging classroom* (5th ed.). Belmont, Ca: Wadsworth.

Gayle-Evans, G. (2004). It is never too soon: A study of kindergarten teachers' implementation of multicultural education in Florida's classrooms. *The Professional Educator, 26*(2), 1-15.

Gerber, S. B., Finn, J. D., Achilles, C. M., & Boyd-Zaharias, J. (2001). Teacher aides and students' academic achievement. *Education Evaluation and Policy Analysis, 23*(2), 123-143.

Gilliam, W. S. (2005). *Prekindergarteners left behind: Expulsion rates in state prekindergarten systems.* New Haven, CT: Yale University Child Study Center.

Goddard, R. D., Hoy, W. K., Woolfolk Hoy, A. (2004). Collective efficacy beliefs: Theoretical developments, empirical evidence, and future directions. *Educational Researcher, 33*, 3-13.

Goleman, D. (2006). *Emotional intelligence: Why it can matter more than IQ* (10th Anniversary ed.). New York: Bantam.

Gray, C., & Garand, J. (1993). Social stories: Improving responses of students with autism with accurate social information. *Focus on Autistic Behavior, 8*(1), 1-10.

Gray, C. (2000). *The new social story book*. Arlington, TX: Future Horizons.

Greenfield, P. (1994). Independence and interdependence as cultural scripts. In P. Greenfield & R. Cocking (Eds.), *Cross-cultural roots of minority child development* (pp. 1-40). Mahwah, NJ: Erlbaum.

Greenfield, P., Keller, H., Fuligni, A., & Maynard, A. (2003). Cultural pathways through universal development. *Annual Review of Psychology, 54,* 461-490.

Gurian, M., & Stevens, K. (2010). *Boys and girls learn differently: A guide for teachers and parents* (10th ed.). San Francisco: Jossey-Bass.

Hall, E. T. (1977). *Beyond culture*. Garden City, NY: Anchor Press/Doubleday.

Han, H. S. & Thomas, M. S. (2010). No child misunderstood: Enhancing early childhood teachers' multicultural responsiveness to the social competence of diverse children. *Early Childhood Education Journal, 37,* 469-476.

Hanley, G. P., Iwata, B. A., & McCord, B. E. (2003). Functional analysis of problem behavior: A review. *Journal of Applied Behavior Analysis, 36*(2), 147-185.

Harriott, W. A., & Martin, S. S. (2004). Using culturally responsive activities to promote social competence and classroom community. *Teaching Exceptional Children, 37*(1), 48-54.

Harrison, Y, & Horne, J. (2000). The impact of sleep deprivation on decision-making: A review. *Journal of Experimental Psychology: Applied, 6*(3), 236-249.

Hastings, R. P. (2003). The relationship between student behaviour patterns and teacher burnout *School Psychology International, 24*(1), 115-127.

Hawken, L. S., Vincent, C. G., & Schumann, J. (2008). Response to Intervention for social behavior: Challenges and opportunities. *Journal of Emotional and Behavioral Disorders, 16*(4), 213-225.

Hayes, R. (2005). Conversation, negotiation, and the word as deed: Linguistic interaction in a dual language program. *Linguistics and Education, 16,* 93-112.

Helmke, A, & Schrader, F. (1988). Successful student practice during seatwork: Efficient management and active supervision not enough. *Journal of Educational Research, 82,* 70-75.

Hemmeter, M. L., Ostrosky, M., & Fox, L. (2006). Social and emotional foundations for early learning: A conceptual model for intervention. *School Psychology Review, 35*(4), 583-601.

Hemmeter, M. L., Ostrosky, M., Santos, R. M., & Joseph, G. (2006). Promoting children's success: Building relationships and creating supportive environments: Center on the Social and Emotional Foundations for Early Learning.

Henderson, A. T., & Mapp, K. L. (2002). A new wave of evidence: The impact of school, family and community connections on student achievement. Annual Synthesis 2002. National Center for Family & Community Connections with Schools (Ed.). Austin, TX: Southeast Educational Development Laboratory.

Hohmann, M., Weikart, D. P., & Epstein, A. S. (2002). *Educating young children* (3rd ed.). Ypsilanti, MI: High Scope Press.

Hughes, J. N., & Kwok, O. (2006). Classroom engagement mediates the effect of teacher-student support on elementary students' peer acceptance: A prospective analysis. *Journal of School Psychology, 43*(6), 465-480.

Irvine, J. J. (2002). African American teachers' culturally specific pedagogy: The collective stories. In J. J. Irvine (Ed.), *In search of wholeness: African American teachers and their culturally specific teacher practices* (pp. 139-146). New York: Palgrave McMillan.

Isaacs, M., & Benjamin, M. (1991). *Towards a culturally competent system of care, volume II: Programs which utilize culturally competent principles*. Washington, D.C: Georgetown University Child

Development Center, CASSP Technical Assistance Center.

Ivey, M. L., Heflin, L. J., & Alberto, P. (2004). The use of Social Stories to promote independent behaviors in novel events for children with PDD-NOS. *Focus on Autism and Other Developmental Disabilities, 19*(3), 149-160.

Iwata, B. A., Dorsey, M. F., Slifer, K. J., Bauman, K. E., & Richman, G. S. (1982). Toward a functional analysis of self-injury. *Journal of Applied Behavior Analysis, 27*, 197-209.

Jennings, P. A., & Greenberg, M. T. (2009). The prosocial classroom: Teacher social and emotional competence in relation to student and classroom outcomes. *Review of Educational Research, 79*(1), 491-525.

Johnson, D. W., & Johnson, R. (1989). *Cooperation and competition: Theory and research*. Edina, MN: Interaction Book Company.

Jones, K., Evans, C., Byrd, R., Campbell, K. . (2000). Gender equity training and teaching behavior. *Journal of Instructional Psychology, 27*(3), 173-178.

Joseph, G. E., & Strain, P. S. (2006). Building positive relationships with young children. *The Center on the Emotional and Social Foundations of Early Learning.* University of Illinois at Urbana-Champaign.

Jung, S., Sainato, D. M., & Davis, C. A. (2008). Using high-probability request sequences to increase social interactions in young children with autism. *Journal of Early Intervention, 30*(3), 163-187.

Kaiser, B., & Rasminsky, J. S. (2007). *Challenging behavior in young children: Understanding, preventing and responding effectively* (2nd ed.). Boston: Pearson.

Katz, K. (2007). *The color of us.* New York: Holt.

Katz, P. A. (2003). Racists or tolerant multiculturalists? How do they begin? *American Psychologist, 58*(11), 897-909.

Kaufman, C. (2010). *Executive function in the classroom: practical strategies for improving performance and enhancing skills for all students.* Baltimore: Paul H. Brookes.

Kirmani, M. H. & Laster, B. P. (1999). Responding to religious diversity in classrooms. *Educational Leadership, 55*(7), 61-63.

Knopf, H. T., & Swick, K. J. (2007). How parents feel about their child's teacher/school: Implications for early childhood professionals. *Early Childhood Education Journal, 34*(4), 291-296.

Kohn, A. (1993). *Punished by rewards.* Boston: Houghton Mifflin.

Kohn, A. (2006). *The homework myth: Why our kids get too much of a bad thing.* New York: De Capo Press.

Kounin, J. (1970). *Discipline and group management in classrooms.* New York: Holt, Rinehart & Winston.

Kume, T., Tokui, A., Hasegawa, N. & Kodama, K.. (2000). *A comparative study of communication styles among Japanese, Americans, and Chinese: Toward an understanding of cultural friction.* Retrieved February 8, 2010, from http://coe-sun.kuis.ac.jp/public/paper/kuis/kume3.pdf

Landrum, T. J., & Kauffman, J. M. (2006). Behavioral approaches to classroom management. In C. M. Evertson & C. S. Weinstein (Eds.), *Handbook of classroom management: Research, practice, and contemporary issues* (pp. 47-71). New York: Routledge.

Lemov, D. (2010). *Teach like a champion: 49 techniques that put students on the path to college.* San Francisco: Jossey-Bass.

Lentini, R. (2004). *I can use my words.* Retrieved January 5, 2009, from http://www.vanderbilt.edu/csefel/scriptedstories/words.ppt

Linehan, M. (1993). *Skills training manual for treating borderline personality disorder*. New York: Guilford Press.

Lortie, D. (2002). *Schoolteacher: A sociological study with a new preface*. Chicago: University of Chicago Press.

Lyman, F. (1981). The responsive classroom discussion. In A. S. Anderson (Ed.), *Mainstreaming Digest*. College Park, MD: University of Maryland College of Education.

Marshall, C.S., Reihartz, J. (1997). Gender issues in the classroom. *Clearinghouse, 70*(6), 333-338.

Marzano, R. J., Marzano, J. S., , & Pickering, D. J. . (2003). *Classroom management that works*. Alexandra, VA: ASCD.

Maslach, C., & Schaufeli, W. B. (1993). Historical and conceptual development of burnout. In C. Maslach, W. B. Schaufeli & T. Marek (Eds.), *Professional burnout: Recent developments in theory and research* (pp. 1-16). Washington, DC: Taylor & Francis.

Maslow, A. H. (1943). A theory of human motivation. *Psychological Review, 50*, 370-396.

Maslow, A. H. (1971). *The farther reaches of human nature*. New York: Viking Press.

Maslow, A. H. (1968). *Toward a psychology of being*. Princeton, NJ: Van Nostrand.

Maslow, A. H. (1999). *Toward a psychology of being, 3rd Edition*. New York: Wiley.

Matheny, K. B., Gfroerer, C. A., & Harris, K. (200). Work stress, burnout, and coping at the turn of the century: An Adlerian perspective. *Journal of Individual Psychology, 56*(1), 74-87.

Matson, J. L., & Minshawi, N. F. (2007). Functional assessment of challenging behavior: Toward a strategy for applied settings. *Research in Developmental Disabilities, 28*, 353-361.

McIntosh, K., Herman, K., Sanford, A., McGraw, K., & Florence, K. (2004). Teaching transitions: Techniques for promoting success *between* lessons. *Teaching Exceptional Children, 37*(1), 32-28.

Miller, K. (2006-2012). *Less is more: Reduce rules and structure to free the minds of boys*. Retrieved from http://www.education.com/reference/article/Ref_Less_More_Reduce/

Miller, M. (2011). Understanding depression. *A Harvard Medical School Special Health Report*. Cambridge, MA: Harvard Medical School.

Minami, M. (2002). *Culture-specific language styles: The development of oral narrative and literacy*. Clevedon, UK: Multilingual Matters.

Mischel, W., Shoda, Y., & Rodriguez, M.I. (1989). Delay of gratification in children. *Science, 244*(4907), 933-938.

Montgomery, C., & Rupp, A. A. (2005). A meta-analysis for exploring the diverse causes and effects of stress in teachers. *Canadian Journal of Education, 28*, 458-486.

Moore, G.T. (1996). A question of privacy: Places to pause and child caves. *Child Care Information Exchange, 112*, 91-95.

Morgan, J., & Ashbaker, B. Y. (2001). *A teacher's guide to working with paraeducators and other classroom aides*. Alexandria, VA: Association for Supervision and Curriculum Development.

Morrow, L. M., & Rand, M. K. (1994). *Physical and social contexts for motivating reading and writing: The WRAP Program. Instructional Resource No. 5, Spring*. Athens, GA: National Reading Research Center.

Moxley, R. A. (1998). Treatment-only designs and student self-recording as strategies for public school teachers. *Education and Treatment of Children, 21*, 37-61.

Mueller, P. H., & Murphy, F. V. (2001). Determining when a student needs paraeducator support. *Teaching Exceptional Children, 33*(6), 22-27.

Mulrine, A. (2001). Are boys the weaker sex? *U.S. News & World Report, 131*(4), 40-48.

Najavits, L. M. (2002). *Seeking safety*. New York: Guilford.

National Education Association. (2002-2010). *Research spotlight on homework.* Retrieved July 6, 2010, from http://www.nea.org/tools/16938.htm

Ogbu, J. (1991). Minority responses and school experiences. *Journal of Psychohistory, 18*, 433-456.

Ogbu, J. (Ed.). (2008). *Minority status, oppositional culture, & schooling (Sociocultural, Political, and Historical Studies in Education)*. New York: Routledge.

Okagaki, L., & Diamond, K. E. (2003). Responding to cultural and linguistic differences in the beliefs and practices of families with young children. In C. Copple (Ed.), *A world of difference: Readings on teaching young children in a diverse society*. Washington, DC: National Association for the Education of Young Children.

Okagaki, L., & Sternberg, R. (1993). Parental beliefs and children's school performance. *Child Development, 52*, 413-429.

Olson, M. R., Chalmers, L., & Hoover, J. H. (1997). Attitudes and attributes of general education teachers identified as effective inclusionists. *Remedial and Special Education, 18*(1), 28-33.

Osher, D., Sprague, J., Weissberg, R. P., Axelrod, J., Keenan, S., Kendziora, K., et al. (2008). A comprehensive approach to promoting social, emotional, and academic growth in contemporary schools. In A. Thomas & J. Grimes (Eds.), *Best practices in school psychology* (5th ed., Vol. 5, pp. 1263–1278). Bethesda, MD: National Association of School Psychologists.

Paley, V. (1993). *You can't say you can't play*. Cambridge, MA: Harvard University Press.

Parker, W. C. (2001). Classroom discussion: Models for leading seminars and deliberations. *Social Education, 65*(2), 111-115.

Patall, E. A., Cooper, H., & Robinson, J. C. (2008). Parent involvement in homework: A research synthesis. *Review of Educational Research, 78*(4), 1039–1101.

Pfister, M. (1992). *The rainbow fish*. New York: North South Books.

Pomerantz, E. M., Moorman, E. A., & Litwack, Scott D. (2007). The how, whom, and why of parents' involvement in children's academic lives: More is not always better. *Review of Educational Research, 77*(3), 373-410.

Ponitz, C. C., McClelland, M. M., Matthews, J. S., & Morrison, F. J. (2009). A structured observation of behavioral self-regulation and its contribution to kindergarten outcomes. *Developmental Psychology, 45*(3), 605-619.

Public Agenda. (2000). *Questionnaire and full survey results: National poll of parents of public school students*. New York: Author.

Quilty, K. M. (2007). Teaching paraprofessionals how to write and implement social stories for students with autism spectrum disorders. *Remedial and Special Education, 28*(3), 182-189.

Responsive Classroom. (2007). *Time Out in a Responsive Classroom (Video)*. Turners Fall, MA: Northeast Foundation for Children.

Reynolds, E. (2006). *Guiding young children: A problem solving-solving approach* (4th ed.). Boston: McGraw Hill.

Rightmyer, E. C. (2003). Democratic discipline: Children creating solutions. *Young Children, 58*(4), 38-45.

Rothbart, M. K., & Bates, J. E. (2006). Temperament in children's development. In R. L. W. Damon, & N. Eisenberg (Ed.), *Handbook of child psychology. Volume 3, Social, emotional, and personality development* (6th ed., pp. 99-153). New York: Wiley.

Ryan, A. L., Halsey, H. N., & Matthews, W. J. (2003). Using functional assessment to promote desirable student behavior in schools. *Teaching Exceptional Children, 35*(5).

Sadker, D., & Sadker, M. (1994) *Failing at fairness: How our schools cheat girls*. Toronto: Simon & Schuster, Inc.

Scheuermann, B., & Hall, J. (2012). *Positive behavioral supports for the classroom* (2nd ed.). Upper Saddle River, NJ: Pearson.

Schneider, N., & Goldstein, H. (2009). Social Stories improve the on-task behavior of children with language impairment. *Journal of Early Intervention, 31*(3), 250-264.

Scullion, T. (n.d.). Collaborative teaching. Retrieved May 17, 2010, from http://www.wjcc.k12.va.us/jbms/FACULTY/ScullionTim/Types%20of%20Collaborative%20Teaching.pdf

Shippen, M. E., Simpson, R. G., & Crites, S. A. (2003). A practical guide to functional behavioral assessment. *Teaching Exceptional Children, 35*(5), 36-44.

Slavin, R. E. (1994). *Cooperative Learning: Theory, research and practice* (2nd ed.). Boston: Allyn & Bacon.

Sridhar, D., & Vaughn, S. (2000). Bibliotherapy for all. *Teaching Exceptional Children, 33*(2), 74-83.

Starkey, P., & Klein, A. (2000). Fostering parental support for children's mathematical development: An intervention with Head Start families. *Early Education and Development, 11*(5), 659-680.

Starr, L. (2005). Meeting *with* the parents: Making the most of parent-teacher conferences. *Education World*. Retrieved January 8, 2010, from http://www.educationworld.com/a_curr/TM/WS_curr291_conf3.shtml

Sugai, G., Horner, R. H., Dunlap, G., Hieneman, M., Lewis, T. J., Nelson, C. M.,...Wilcox, B. (1999). Applying positive behavioral support and functional behavior assessment in schools. Washington, D.C.: OSEP Center on Positive Behavioral Interventions and Support.

Tabors, P. (2004). What early childhood educators need to know: Developing effective programs for linguistically and culturally diverse children and families. In C. Copple (Ed.), *A world of difference: Readings on teaching young children in a diverse society*. Washington, D.C.: National Association for the Education of Young Children.

Tangney, J. P., & Dearing, R. L. (2002). *Shame and guilt*. New York: Guilford Press.

Tannen, D. (2001). *You just don't understand: Men and women in conversation* (New paperback ed.). New York: Quill.

The IRIS Center for Training Enhancements. (n.d.-a). *Addressing disruptive and noncompliant behaviors (part 1): Understanding the acting-out cycle.* Retrieved April 21, 2010, from http://iris.peabody.vanderbilt.edu/bi1/cresource.htm

The IRIS Center for Training Enhancements. (n.d.-b). *Addressing disruptive and noncompliant behaviors (part 2): Behavioral interventions.* Retrieved January 4, 2010, from http://iris.peabody.vanderbilt.edu/bi2/chalcycle.htm

The IRIS Center for Training Enhancements. (n.d.-d). *Who's in charge? Developing a comprehensive behavior management system.* Retrieved December 1, 2009, from http://iris.peabody.vanderbilt.edu/parmod/chalcycle.htm

Thompson, R. A. (1994). Emotional regulation: A theme in search of a definition. In N. A. Fox (Ed.), *The development of emotional regulation: Biological and behavioral considerations* (Vol. 59, pp. 25-52): Monographs of the Society for Research in Child Development.

Tobin, K. (1987). The role of wait time in higher cognitive level learning. *Review of Educational Research, 57*(1), 69-95.

Torres-Guzman, M. (1998). Language culture, and literacy in Puerto Rican communities. In B. Perez (Ed.), *Sociocultural contexts of language and literacy*. Mahwah, NJ: Erlbaum.

Tsouloupas, C., Carson, R., Matthews, R., Grawitch, M., & Barber, L. (2010). Exploring the association between teachers' perceived student misbehaviour and emotional exhaustion: The importance of teacher efficacy beliefs and emotion regulation. *Educational Psychology, 30*(2), 173-189.

U.S. Department of Education National Center for Education Statistics. (2001). *The kindergarten year: Findings from the Early Childhood Longitudinal Study, Kindergarten Class or 1998-99 (NCES 2001-023)*. Washington, D.C.: Author.

Viorst, J. (2009). *Alexander and the terrible, horrible, no good, very bad day*. New York: Atheneum.

Voorhis, V. (2004). Reflecting on the homework ritual: Assignments and designs. *Theory into Practice, 43*(3), 205-212.

Vygotsky, L. (1978). *Mind in society: the development of higher psychological processes*. Cambridge, MA: Harvard University Press.

Wallace, T., Shin, J., Bartholomay, T., & Stahl, B. J. (2001). Knowledge and skills for teachers supervising the work of paraprofessionals. *Exceptional Children, 67*(4), 520-533.

Walsh, B. A., & Blewitt, P. (2006). The effect of questioning style during storybook reading on novel vocabulary acquisition of preschoolers. *Early Childhood Education Journal, 33*(4), 273-278.

Wardle, F. (2004). Supporting multiracial and multiethnic children and their families. In C. Copple (Ed.), *A world of difference: Readings on teaching young children in a diverse society*. Washington, D.C.: National Association for the Education of Young Children.

Ware, F. (2002). Black teachers' perceptions of their professional roles and practices. In J. J. Irvine (Ed.), *In search of wholeness: African American teachers and their culturally specific classroom practices* (pp. 33-46). New York: Palgrave.

Ware, F. (2006). Warm demander pedagogy: Culturally responsive teaching that supports a culture of achievement for African American students. *Urban Education, 41*(4), 427-456.

Webster-Stratton, C. (1991). *The teachers and children videotape series: Dina dinosaur school*. Seattle, WA: The Incredible Years.

Weinstein, C. S. (1991). The classroom as social context for learning. *Annual Review of Psychology, 42*, 492-525.

Weinstein, C. S., & Mignano, A. J. (2006). *Elementary classroom management: Lessons from research and practice*. New York: McGraw-Hill.

Wolfgang, C. H., & Glickman, C. D. (1986). *Solving discipline problems: Strategies for classroom teachers* (2nd ed.). Boston: Allyn & Bacon.

Wong, H, & Wong, R. (2004). *The first days of school: How to be an effective teacher*. Mountain View: Harry K. Wong Publications.

Wood, B. K., Cho Blair, K., & Ferro, J. B. (2009). Young children with challenging behavior: function-based assessment and intervention. *Topics in Early Childhood Special Education, 29*(2), 68-78.

Young, C. (2010). *Narrate the positive*. Retrieved from http://teacherevolution.com/2010/09/13/narrate-the-positive/

About the Author

Muriel K. Rand, is Professor of Early Childhood Education at New Jersey City University. She has spent 20 years working with preschool and elementary teachers in urban public schools. She began her career as a preschool teacher and has been preparing new teachers since 1995. She writes *The Positive Classroom* blog which focuses on classroom management strategies for teachers of young children: www.thepositiveclassroom.org/

Dr. Rand has published two books of teaching cases: *Voices of Student Teachers: Cases from the Field* (Merrill, 2003) and *Giving it Some Thought: Cases for Early Childhood Practice* (NAEYC, 2000). She is also a prolific and successful grant writer. She holds an Ed.D. and an M.S.W. degree from Rutgers University. She can be contacted at murielrand@thepositiveclassroom.org .

About the Illustrator

Catherine L. Rand is a free-lance artist, award-winning sculptor, writer, and film-maker. Her interests include a passion for traveling, learning languages, and history. She has studied in Paris with Rutgers University and in Ireland at University College, Dublin.

Ms. Rand is a member of Phi Beta Kappa and holds a B.A. in Art History and Sculpture from Rutgers University. She is currently completing a Master in Fine Arts at the New York Film Academy.

Made in the USA
Lexington, KY
22 August 2014